SOCIAL MANUAL FOR SEMINARIANS

Social Manual
for Seminarians

REVEREND THOMAS F. CASEY

REVEREND LEO C. GAINOR, O.P.

FOREWORD BY HIS EMINENCE
RICHARD CARDINAL CUSHING

THE BRUCE PUBLISHING COMPANY
Milwaukee

IMPRIMI POTEST:

    J. E. MARR, O.P.
    Provincial

NIHIL OBSTAT:

    MATTHEW P. STAPLETON
    Diocesan Censor

IMPRIMATUR:

    ✠ RICHARD CARDINAL CUSHING
    Archbishop of Boston
    May 29, 1962

Library of Congress Catalog Card Number: 63-14377

© 1963 THE BRUCE PUBLISHING COMPANY
MADE IN THE UNITED STATES OF AMERICA

To
MOST REVEREND THOMAS J. RILEY, D.D., PH.D.
AUXILIARY BISHOP OF BOSTON, FORMER RECTOR,
ST. JOHN'S SEMINARY, BRIGHTON

FOREWORD

Our modern seminarians face a formidable challenge as they generously answer the call of God to lifelong service. Intellectual and moral formation must be achieved during the brief period of their association with the seminary. Many forces within and without the individual candidate combine in assault on his good purpose. Strengthened by the sacraments and guided by his bishop, shaped by the devoted attention of his seminary professors, and encouraged by the loving prayers of his family, the young man labors to reach the goal to which his vocation summons him.

Within the young man lie qualities which the passing years will see develop. He has it in him to become first a gentleman, next an educated priest, and then a saint. One step achieved will lead him to the next and each is necessary for the full realization of the inner qualities bestowed on him by God. Man, gentleman, priest, and saint are the challenging stages of the developing life that lies before the young seminarian.

It is for the development of the gentleman that Father Gainor and Father Casey have composed this manual. As priests speaking to seminarians who share the priestly vocation, they offer guidance in the many social situations encountered by a seminarian. Included are the social responsibilities of the community life of the seminary and the demands of proper behavior which occur when seminarians are on leave from the seminary. The authors examine the social customs as they apply to seminarians, treat of a range of topics and present practical directions for the exemplification of the social graces.

Their theme is charity in action. Recognizing the supremacy of the virtue of charity as do all intelligent followers of Christ, they counsel the application of the virtue of charity to all the situations encountered in daily life. Thus the manual aids in the development of the basic virtue and leads seminarians toward the personification of the Catholic gentleman. No pretense or affectation enters into this role of the Catholic gentleman. The seminarian is shown the connection that exists between good manners and virtue, propriety and manliness. The style is refreshing and should effectively instruct the readers of the manual.

Our seminarians' external manners should be a reflection of their inner motivation, charity in action: love of God and love of neighbor. The love of God has brought these students to our seminaries. The love of neighbor should motivate them to acquire gracious knowledge of correct social relations so as to make their future apostolate more effective. Good manners have immediate results too, in contributing to the happiness of fellow seminarians and maintaining harmonious cooperation among these generous young men. The Christlike seminarian is the ideal and all must strive toward this goal.

May this manual prove helpful to our beloved seminarians as they face the challenge to be gentlemen, educated priests, and, ultimately, saints.

RICHARD CARDINAL CUSHING
Archbishop of Boston

ACKNOWLEDGMENTS

This manual is an outgrowth of a brochure written by Father Gainor which was privately printed and distributed to the Dominican students of his midwest province of St. Albert the Great.

Father Casey has enlarged the text, modified and adapted it for the needs of the minor and major diocesan seminaries of the country. Much of the contents is original. The chapters, for instance on Sports, Waiting on Table, Good Manners in Action, and First Solemn Mass are entirely new.

While the manual itself and the examples, or illustrations used are directed particularly to the diocesan students, the authors have attempted to make the general rules of conduct have equal application to the religious students in their respective novitiates, scholasticates, and houses of studies.

The special gratitude of the authors is extended to Fritz Bamberger, Executive Director of *Esquire* Magazine, for his generous permission to use material from the recent copyrighted book *New Esquire Etiquette for Men*. The chapters on smoking and eating are almost exact reproductions of the original *Esquire Etiquette* text.

Also thanks is extended to the Very Reverend Francis J. Connell, C.Ss.R., Catholic University of America, Washington, D. C., for permission to quote extensively from his pamphlet *The Gentlemanly Priest*.

Special thanks are given to the officers of various diocesan seminaries who read the original manuscript and offered valuable comments and suggestions which were incorporated in the final copy.

To the literary experts, who wish to conceal themselves behind the veil of anonymity; to the editorial staff of the Bruce Publishing Company, particularly to William Straub who has patiently followed the development of this work through many months and for his expert guidance and encouragement during difficult times; to all those who helped with the typing of the copy and the proofreading of the galley sheets; to all who helped by deed or word to make this effort a reality; to all these the authors publicly acknowledge their indebtedness and extend their profound thanks.

May the hope also be expressed that all these helpers may be rewarded through the cordial reception by the seminarians of this little book of conduct rules, and that it may prove helpful to them toward establishing patterns of gracious living for their future priestly ministrations.

THE AUTHORS

INTRODUCTION

Purpose

This manual is intended to be helpful to the young men who are aspiring to the priesthood in the Catholic Church. It is, if you wish to so label it, "A Textbook on Clerical Etiquette." It is designed to be indicative rather than comprehensive.

In its purpose, however, it goes beyond the mere cataloguing of general rules and regulations of social conduct, and visualizes you, the future priest, as a sum total of all your training — spiritual, moral, intellectual, physical, and social. The resulting composite is the ordained priest — a cultured Catholic gentleman. This book covers only one phase of that training or preparation: the social proprieties.

Terms Explained

"Cultured Catholic Gentleman," as we use the term, signifies the Catholic priest who is motivated by charity, by love of God, and by love of neighbor. His life is a life of service to God and his fellowman. This culture expresses itself in all his human relations.

St. Thomas Aquinas, with his great acumen, calls this quality "affability," the ability to get along amicably with our fellowmen. The key thought then, as now, was consideration and thoughtfulness for others.

St. Thomas attributes this quality of affability, or friendliness, to the virtue of justice. He says in part:

> This virtue of affability is a part of Justice, being joined to it as to a principal virtue . . . (for example: the branch to the tree). Affability regards a certain debt of equity, namely, that we behave pleasantly toward those among whom we dwell. Therefore, it behooves us to exercise a certain regard towards others in our mutual relations, both in deeds and in words, so that we behave towards each other in an agreeable manner. Hence, the need of a special virtue that maintains this harmony of relationship. This virtue we call "friendliness" (Q. 114, 115; Part II–II).

So St. Thomas recognized that affability and friendliness are closely allied to good manners and to consideration of the rights of others. He makes only one exception, which we can readily accept with its implications:

> Unless at times, for some reason, it is necessary to displease others for some good purpose.

Your Regulations

All seminaries, major and minor, lay down the same rule for their students. The wording may vary but the central idea is the same everywhere: the motivation of social conduct is *charity;* charity in action; charity in love for God and love for neighbor.

The seminarian becomes a priest out of love of God, but love of neighbor stimulates him to effective ministry through conformity to the accepted social code and through facility in his human relations.

It is an essential part of your apostolate that you acquire good manners in order to secure the respect of the public and the confidence of the laity.

The general public expects you, and rightly so, to have a certain affability in your behavior, combined with modesty and graciousness. Anything short of this will startle the people and reflect unfavorably upon your ministry.

Habit-Forming Time

Clerical students start off with a handicap, however. You, the future priest, must spend many of your formative years practically isolated from normal social contacts with active society. You enter the minor seminary in your teens. You spend additional years of training largely removed from the influence of your family, home life, and mixed society.

Unlike young men in high school, college, or in the business world, you have little opportunity to realize that your attitudes and social deportment make a distinct impression upon the people with whom you come into contact. Your affability and courtesy create your "image" in the public mind.

It is during these secluded years of collegiate, philosophical, and theological study that you are trained in the social graces. But your opportunities to put them into practice are somewhat limited. Therefore, make the most of every occasion among your classmates; in your own family circle; toward people who come to the seminary; on visiting Sundays; during vacation periods.

If you are not alert and do not give close attention to the social conventions during this period of time, you will undoubtedly develop graceless, plebeian, or even offensive manners. These undesirable traits will correspondingly impede your effective service during your active years of ministry. It is a rule of society, a fact of life, that persons are judged by externals. You will not be exempted from this critical appraisal.

Judgment by Others

Your personal appearance, student or young priest, your bearing, tact, poise, your courtesy in dealings with others, your awareness and observance of social conventions — all these factors make a favorable or a disagreeable impression upon others. Moreover, these judgments are formed even before your other qualities are considered, such as knowledge, intelligence, or your moral character. You will be appraised according to these external standards and there isn't anything you can do about it except to conform to the code.

Final Determinant

Common sense must be the final factor which governs your application of conventional rules to particular circumstances in your social life as a young priest. Just one example will illustrate this point. It is a rule that we shake hands with the right hand. Imagine the confusion that would result if this rule was not generally followed! Yet, there are many particular circumstances, for instance, with the handicapped, or the man with painful arthritis, where this rule cannot be applied. Hence you must make "common sense" the ultimate criterion of proper usage.

You have one broad general rule — to smooth the troubled waters of social convention — and to give you confidence and assurance in your approach. It is contained implicitly, at least, in your regulations: your spiritual and theological training is a preparation for your harvest of souls; so too, is your gentlemanly training a preparation for life situations; for your charity in action — the salvation of souls.

You must make use of all natural means, as well as spiritual ones, in your apostolate. If externals of dress, deportment, and observances of customs are weighty factors in influencing others, then they must become important elements in your apostolate.

Thus, you as a priest will take your rightful place with the cultured people of the world. These people will recognize that you are in the world, but not of the world. You will take your place in the classroom, the college, the university, in the parish, on the lecture platform, in the pulpit, in the Church societies — wherever cultured and intellectual men and women gather. You will be observed, on inspection wherever you appear. You must not disappoint these people.

Inspirational Example

You should take your inspiration from Christ Himself who never was guilty of a breach of politeness. Christ in His public life praised some and rebuked others when it was necessary, but on all occasions He was courteous. He never willingly inflicted pain on any man, but He rebuked those who forgot their manners. There was the time when Christ upbraided Simon, the Pharisee, at his table, when he neglected to perform the ordinary courtesies of the day for Christ, his guest — the washing, the anointing, the kiss of peace; yet at that same table Christ gently lifted the penitent Magdalene from the depth of shame to the heights of sanctity.

Christ was on easy terms with the rich and poor alike. He could go hungry with His Apostles, eat with sinners, or dine at the table of the rich Zacchaeus. He could find rest on the roadside or sleep in the home of His friend Lazarus. He worked His first miracle to save embarrassment to the newly-weds. He was all things to all men, and in all His human relations He was ever the cultured gentleman. He is the perfect model for your imitation.

CONTENTS

xviii   CONTENTS

SOCIAL MANUAL FOR SEMINARIANS

Let no man despise thy youth, but
be thou an example to the faithful
in speech, in conduct, in charity,
in faith, in chastity (1 Tim 4:12).

Chapter 1. PROPER TRAINING

Your Personal Cleanliness

The foundation of your personal appearance is cleanliness of your person. Fortunately for you, your homes, your colleges, and your seminaries provide ample facilities for your personal grooming.

Under these favorable conditions it becomes exceedingly difficult for you to offer a valid excuse for giving offense to others by body odors, irrespective of how violent your physical exercise in sports, or your expenditure of energy in other activities. You can't blame it on the weather conditions, for your companions endure the same heat waves. While they may not say anything, they will not accept your implied excuses.

Rigid Custom

This point of etiquette is equally true of other thorough cleanliness factors. We are rapidly becoming a people inexorably dedicated to immaculateness of person and dress. As a result we are increasingly intolerant of those who either deliberately, or inadvertently, flaunt these conventions. We will not accept excuses.

Thanks to newspaper and magazine advertisements and to TV commercials regarding soaps, deodorants, toothpastes, and mouthwashes you scarcely need to be reminded here of the importance of daily baths, the use of deodorants, the necessity of regular teeth brushing, close shaves, the assurance

1

of fresh, clean breath, frequent shampoos, clean fingernails, and fresh linens. If you are meticulous and regular now in observing these regulations they will become habitual and you can always feel confident of your presentability under all circumstances.

Specifications of Canon Law

The sacred Canons of the Church recognize these hygienic regulations and insist upon their observance. The Church law also recommends propriety in dress and in manners. It places the responsibility upon the seminary officials for stressing these rules to the seminarians, and for giving good example themselves in these matters of decorum.

Canon 1369, paragraph 2 reads:

> (The seminary officials) shall frequently stress the rules of true Christian etiquette and stimulate the seminarians by example to the cultivation of them; morever the officials shall urge the seminarians to the scrupulous observance of hygienic demands of cleanliness of body and in dress; and of a certain geniality combined with modesty and dignity in conversation.

Practice Makes Perfect

The seminary, as Canon Law recognizes, is the proper place to acquire these desirable habits of neatness and personal grooming. This entire treatise, SOCIAL MANUAL FOR SEMINARIANS, might be considered a development and expansion of this particular Canon 1369, for as the Church recognizes, in this entire field of personal cleanliness it becomes a matter of constant vigilance for you to keep yourself presentable. However the practice will pay dividends, for such habits acquired as a student, under the inspiration and example of the seminary officials, will remain with you throughout your active ministry.

Practical Application

By way of practical illustration, take such matter-of-fact things as your hair and your fingernails. What will be said of them here applies with equal force to other qualities of personal cleanliness. These two examples are used merely to emphasize the surveillance required in this entire field of personal appearance.

In respect to your hair, if you have it, be thankful, and keep it well groomed. The hair is a key item in your appearance, so get your hair cut every two weeks. Do not affect the extreme styles, the bizarre effects, the "prison" cut, or the flashy combings of the ultramodern youth. Any indulgence or affectation in any of these styles, or combings, will immediately forfeit your companions' good opinions and merit censure from your superiors.

If your hair has vanished, or is disappearing, as sometimes happens during seminary days and more frequently in active years, accept the inevitable (now and later) with masterful sangfroid. Do not attempt ingenious methods of combing, nor try to make a few long hairs cover the tonsured spots. You will only advertise your painful consciousness of an irremediable condition. Take what comfort you can in what Shakespeare makes Dromio say in the *Comedy of Errors*: "What Time hath scanted men in hair he hath given them in wit." And remember you have much company with your baldish pate.

Have a regular day every second week for barbering. Have the barber trim the eyebrows and ears if they require it. Do not get exotic trims, nor have the barber clip the hair close to the scalp. Then take care of your hair by proper weekly shampoo and regular hair dressing of your own preference.

In respect to your fingernails, if you develop the habit of

keeping them trimmed and shaped the process will become almost automatic. However, do not cut the nails straight across, or down to the quick. Keep the nails rounded (not pointed) and curved as nature intended. Of course, keep them clean at all times.

If you have developed the childish habit of biting your fingernails, or chewing off hangnails with your teeth, break it at once! Most people have a horror at witnessing such a performance.

Keep a manicure set, or at least a pair of manicure scissors and a nail file, among your toilet accessories. It is fallacious thinking to consider the practice effeminate.

Your Clothing

Neatness of attire is a correlative of cleanliness of body. It is an acquired habit. The prospective priest is not a fop, nor a fashion plate; neither does he affect the effeminate, nor the eccentric.

Your attire, whether clerical or civilian clothes, should be neat and clean. Street trousers should be pressed. Shoes should be polished at all times. Remember Shaw's *Pygmalion* (and *My Fair Lady*): "He's a gentleman; look at his boots."

Black socks should be worn with black shoes, never white or colored socks . . . the clashing contrast is out of place for clergymen. And, speaking of socks, they should be of the "stretch" variety which cling to the legs . . . resort to garters if necessary . . . for the sight of socks draping down on ankles has a disturbingly "undress" effect.

Practice: Again get in the habit of proper grooming and it will become almost automatic. For instance, polish the shoes each day, or at least give them a cloth brushing. Do this at a regular time, say when you return to your room after Mass and breakfast.

Watch out for your cassocks. Inspect them regularly. Do not permit them to become stained with perspiration bands under the armpits. Inspect them frequently for spots on the underside of sleeves; watch for frayed cuffs, loose hooks, protruding Roman collars sticking up in the back.

Confine your loafer shoes and sandals to your own room. When on the street keep coat properly buttoned. Do not be an "odd ball" in wearing out-of-date street clothing. Spats went out with grandfather; derbies with father; double-breasted suits in your own time. The vest has practically gone, and the white scarf is going. So conform. If and when these styles come back — conform. Pope's advice applies here: "In words, as fashions . . ."

> Be not the first by whom the new are tried,
> Nor yet the last to lay the old aside.

Cassocks and street clothing should be kept clean with spots removed at once. Linen wear and clerical collars should be spotlessly clean. It is not a matter of financial economy to wear your white composition collar until it is as yellow as a canary. Some seminarians affect the "Joe College" type. They don't seem to grow out of their varsity days. Remember Shakespeare said: "The apparel oft proclaims the man" (*Hamlet*, Act 1).

To sum up: Slovenliness in dress, either in the seminary, classroom, or on the street, is a mark of carelessness unbecoming a gentleman. At the other extreme is fastidiousness — the soft, unmanly type with distaff tendencies and effeminate touches. This is unbecoming an aspirant to the priesthood.

A Warning

So you can "overdress" or "underdress." There is a proper time and a proper place for certain types of clothes, such as the formal civilian dress, the sports clothing, the attire for school hikes. The caution here is: Beware of too much informality.

There is a proper place for your T-shirts and your sweat shirts; for your loafer shoes and your sandals; for your "fatigue" clothing and your sneakers . . . but there are two warning alarms: Don't overdo it; and don't do it at the wrong time or place. For instance, don't answer the front doorbell or go to the parlor in your T-shirt.

We must face the fact that the T-shirt is here to stay; that it is easy to handle; that it is comfortable; that it does save laundry labor; but it hasn't entirely replaced the long sleeves. The correct wear for altar services and preaching is white shirt with long sleeves. Confine the use of the T-shirt more properly for "home" wear.

Just one more example may help to clarify this point. When community walks are taken by the students on hikes in the country, the informal clothing should not approximate the "hobo-type." You are a group of religious students, not an unsupervised class of juvenile schoolboys. You can enjoy comfort and informality in your dress without giving the impression to passersby or neighborhood residents that you are escapees from a detention camp. In a word, your dress and behavior should be mature.

Your Obligation

It follows, therefore, that you owe it to yourself and to your diocese to dress properly on all occasions. If you believe that "clothes make the man," dress so that your clothes will give that impression. Offbeat clothes will give an offbeat impression.

Your clothes — like your manners — are apt to be taken as a key to your character. It's a foolish criterion, on the face of it; but on the face of it, what other criterion has the passing public to judge you by in this frenetic world of first impressions? How is the public to judge on these community walks, for example, or at sports events, that you are religious students and not a teen-age gang?

You are probably more or less familiar with the Rule of St. Augustine. He sums up this topic in this manner:

> Avoid singularity in dress, and strive to please others by your conduct and not by your clothes. Let there be nothing to offend the eyes of anyone, either in your gait, your posture, your dress, or your movements, but let everything about you be in keeping with the holiness of your state.

(NOTE: If you have any doubts as to the propriety of your clothing, a good rule is to consult one or two of your companions. They will readily inform you, but not unless you ask them.)

Practice: It is a good rule always to wear suit or cassock when on the "job." If you get accustomed to T-shirt wear as a regular practice, when you are in the parish you will probably follow the same habit. You will meet people at the rectory door in a T-shirt!

Just one last word on this subject. Your clothes are entitled to proper care. Don't hang your coat on a hook in the wardrobe. You won't see the indentation of the hook in the back of your coat collar, but everybody else will! Use a wooden hanger to keep the coat in proper shape and use pants hangers to drape the trousers.

Your Room

In major seminaries ordinarily each student has his own private room which he cares for himself. In college, rooms sometimes are shared, but the responsibility for their condition rests upon the occupants.

Your room will reflect your habits and to some degree your mind. A fair appraisal can be made of you from the contents and the condition of your room.

If you wish to keep "out of the hair" of the superior, and incidentally develop good housekeeping traits, you will air your room daily, and keep it clean-swept and neat at all times.

Here are a few obvious hints. Of course, if you are inclined to be careless, or a nonconformist who regards all housekeeping as "woman's work," or if you are a radical who deplores neatness as a sign of weakness, then these tips won't be valued by you. But if you are as eager to improve your room service as you are your golf score or your batting average, then you can check this inventory.

You should make your bed promptly and properly. Use the bedspread if you are provided with one.

Mop and dust daily. Your shoeshine kit (a necessity) should be kept in operative order. Do not use face towels to shine your shoes, nor use bath towels as mops or dust cloths.

Laundry bags or clothes chutes are provided and should be used for soiled linen.

Your clothes should be hung in the closet.

Keep room neat and orderly. Dispose of things not needed. Your desk, table, books, and papers should be systematically grouped, not a jumble of disorderliness. Get accustomed to using paper clips or rubber bands to keep related papers together. Use folders or a file system for permanent records.

If smoking is permitted in the room, the ashes and butts should be deposited in the proper receptacles and these should be emptied daily or more frequently.

The proper place for wastepaper and discarded things is in the wastebasket, not on the floor!

The washstand, if the room is provided with one, should

be spotless at all times; and your toilet accessories should be kept in the cabinet provided for that purpose.

If a community washroom is used, you should leave the washbowl clean and dry for the next person. The same principle applies to common shower baths, soaps, and other accessories. They should be left in proper usable order. It is a mark of discourtesy to do otherwise.

Happy Results

In the military service of our country the officials insist on servicemen being "dressed up" when on public view, and on living quarters being "policed," i.e., neat and orderly. The same standards should apply to those who aspire to service in the priesthood.

If these proper habits of orderliness are acquired during your formative years, two results will inevitably follow when you are assigned to active duty:

1. You will never be embarrassed by your untidy room when the pastor pops in unexpectedly; and the housekeeper will not complain to him regularly about "that young assistant's room."

2. When you stay overnight on your visit to your classmate at his rectory, or at a private home when on vacation, your acquired guest habits will be such that they will bring commendation from the housekeeper and approval of your cultural habits from your hostess.

Chapter 2. POSTURE AND CARRIAGE

Introduction

Closely allied to personal appearance are posture and carriage — the way you walk, stand, and sit.

You can be precisely neat in dress and exacting in cleanliness, yet the whole effect can be ruined by your indifferent posture and your graceless carriage.

In walking, first of all, cultivate a proper conscious attitude toward your bearing. You are not a military man in uniform with shoulders rigid and stride measured; nor an actor with swaggering step; nor a rustic with lumbering gait. You are a man of God with a mission to perform. Walk with the dignity of your calling — with head erect and body relaxed.

Your stride should be a moderate one proportionate to your height. Shoulders should be even, not humped or one higher than the other. The head should be erect, not bobbing or carried to one side; the arm swing should be natural with the hands exposed. The prospective priest does not walk publicly with hands in trousers' pockets.

Finishing schools still use the "book-on-the-head" method for acquiring proper walking posture and for ascending or descending stairs. This mechanical precision is not expected (nor desired) in a priest. Yet, neither should you travel with long strides as though in a walking race, nor mince your steps as though prancing along, nor thump your feet as though shattering the sidewalk. You should carry yourself as becomes your profession. Let your walk be dignified and graceful.

As a child has to be taught to take its first steps, so too you must acquire the proper techniques if you have developed careless habits in walking. There must be a conscious approach to the problem. "Watch your step" is an apt warning here.

Standing

There really is only one simple rule for standing: Keep both of your feet on the floor with your bodily weight fairly evenly divided between them — not rigidly as a military man at attention, but gracefully at ease.

This is the correct position for you at all times, at church services, in classroom, before religious superiors, in the pulpit, with seculars.

Your weight should not be borne by one leg. In the sanctuary (and this is highly important) the back of the chair or the prie-dieu should not be used to support your arms or bodily weight.

Such a slumped, crooked, or slovenly posture in church could easily be interpreted as an indication of your mental attitude toward the recitation of prayers.

Stand erect in the chapel and at church services. Let your hands be joined with fingers extended and together. Put left hand on breast when right hand is in use.

If you acquire this proper bearing in your student days, you can have assurance that you will give edification to the people when you perform your priestly offices.

Sitting

Proper seating means that you sit erect, neither sprawling with extended feet nor slouching with curved back. Both feet should be placed squarely on the floor.

Crossing your legs when you are in a straight-back chair

is today generally accepted, but you will never offend by keeping both feet on the floor.

Chairs, of course, are never tilted back, and feet are not put on the rungs . . . and you should never sit on a desk or table, nor should you place your feet on them.

But in our day with the modern furniture in public places and private homes, you are more or less forced to lounge as you sit. Modern styled sofas and deep-seated chairs present a difficult challenge to you for graceful sitting and a gymnastic problem for arising. The only proposal here is one of sympathy for you when caught in such modern traps and mental support as you try to boost yourself out of them.

Application of Foregoing

If you develop proper carriage and posture, correct walking and sitting, you will have acquired approved habits of conduct and composure for use both in the sacristy and in the church before the public.

So when you are before the public observe these regulations:

1. You will walk quietly and with dignity; you will close doors noiselessly; you will genuflect with hands joined, a straight back and without reaching for support; you will kneel squarely on both knees without half-supporting your body on the rear pew.

2. You will take holy water properly and cross yourself reverently and thoughtfully with left hand flat on breast.

3. You will keep custody of the eyes in church or chapel. You will refrain from scrutinizing the laity. Even in the social code of society it is vulgar to stare at a woman.

4. One rule, easy to remember, sums up the foregoing succinctly in this sentence: "Let there be nothing to offend the eyes of anybody, either in your gait, your posture, your

dress, or your movements, but let everything about you be in keeping with the holiness of your state."

In all this observance you will be preparing yourself for the dignified performance of your public priestly functions.

You may be confident that by this proper demeanor acquired in your student days you will give edification to the people now and when you perform your priestly offices; and you may, thereby, unconsciously, be of use to the soul of your neighbor.

The same suggestion is offered here as under "Clothing." Take a private inventory of the way you walk, stand, and sit. Then if you have any doubts consult one or two of your companions. They will confirm or dispel your doubts, but they won't volunteer this information. You must seek it.

Chapter 3. CONVERSATION

General

For you to be a good conversationalist, strange as it may seem, it is not necessary for you to be a fluent talker.

An essential quality of a conversationalist is that he be a good listener.

You can make this test: If you closely follow the development of the story or the theme being propounded, if you ask leading questions and make appropriate observations, then you are a good listener.

This type of listener makes a positive, active contribution to the conversation, for attentive listening is not a negative quality. It is an intelligent interest in the speaker and his subject matter. It displays scope of knowledge, sympathies, and genuine interest in people.

A good listener is a "rara avis." You will be one in a thousand, a man of mark!

Good Listener

A good listener has the ability to draw out the shy or timid by gently directing the conversation toward the shy one's forte, or aptitude, or knowledge. You can learn by practice.

For instance, almost anyone, artisan or artist, talks well on subjects in which he thinks himself particularly competent, if he feels you are a sympathetic and interested listener. A truck driver, for example, could entertain (or instruct) a sympathetic listener by many road incidents or driving techniques.

Obviously, do not interrupt. There are two kinds of interruption. The more obvious one, interrupting the speaker in midsentence, is easy to avoid; just wait until he has stopped talking before you start. (And never say, "Have you finished?" You might as well say right out "I thought you'd never run down.")

The other kind of interruption, equally culpable, is often prefaced by "that reminds me . . ." or "by the way. . . ." Such interruptions usually signify a digression or an irrelevancy. In any event, you have mortally wounded the conversation. It can never recover.

On the other hand, if you, the speaker, are leading the way, you should be wary of many pitfalls. They can be devastating to intelligent conversation. Some of these deadly traps are given below. Others will readily occur to you, if you are interested in becoming a good conversationalist. Avoiding them may keep you from becoming either a boor or a bore. Someone has aptly said a bore is one who talks about himself when you want to talk about yourself. So see that your "I" has overtones of "you."

Pitfalls

You as a student should manifest a certain maturity and a manly reserve in talking with older people, especially to older priests.

You should not blurt out all you think or know or have heard on your first meetings with the seasoned veterans.

You should not ask senseless questions or feel constrained to keep up a constant chatter. Think before you talk and think beyond the subject at hand. That's the secret of tact.

You should respect the privacy of the older priests — and reserve a little for yourself. Above all, don't go fishing for news. Let them steer the conversation into their own channel.

And, here a little admonition might save you, when you become the young priest, some future embarrassment. Refrain from calling the older priests by their first names, or their nicknames. This familiarity is properly reserved for their classmates, or long-time associates. It is the same principle as your student days — nicknames of your classmates are reserved to your own respective groups.

You must avoid personalities in analyzing the speech or commands of superiors, and avoid attributing improper motives to their judgments, for frequently you will not know all the reasons or circumstances which determine these judgments. This "griping" breeds unhappiness. Such reprehensible talk is not only lacking in social grace but it offends against Christian charity. Exhibit loyalty and *esprit de corps*. If you are trying to make an impression on the older Fathers, you will succeed much better by your naturalness and loyalty than by a critical attitude.

Some Other Cautions

There are some other "Don't's" in conversation which may have particular application to you. You can easily check, privately, of course:

1. Don't correct another's grammar or pronunciation in public, not even indirectly. Even your closest friend will resent it, and properly so. If your purpose is to be helpful and not pedantic, conduct your English lesson in private.

2. Don't say, "Stop me if you've heard this . . ." because no one will ever stop you, even if it is a twice-told tale.

3. Don't say "huh?" or "What?" or "Pardon me?" when you mean "What did you say?" or "Sorry, I didn't hear what you said." And don't use the overworked "Yeah." Also avoid slang words, such as, "guys," "kids," "bucks." These utterances grow on you and they will betray you when least expected!

4. Don't use a lot of Latin words or foreign phrases. All the Fathers and students know your linguistic ability. Don't strain your language to publicize your foreign travels. They will know whether you are Rome bound or just returning.

5. Don't give secondhand opinions or ideas without crediting their source. Sooner or later the idea thief is always caught in the act — and you will lose face. And these final tips:

6. Don't be a "know-it-all," a "show-off," a clown, or a quipster. If you are one of these types you will soon acquire among your more discerning brethren a reputation for superficiality and irresponsibility.

7. Don't constantly remind your bald-headed or your heavier brethren of their plight. They know it. You drive a sharp nail into a tender area. Your hammer can do serious damage.

Positive Aids

There are also the "Do's" as well as the above "Don't's." Here are a few of them for consideration.

Above all, be natural! You've often heard that what you say and how you say it is a first impression giveaway to your character and background. It's a bigger giveaway to pretend to be something you are not than to be what you are without apology. In short, affectation or pretense will ultimately disclose itself — then you will be stark naked! So be natural. Be yourself. Be a man. And you'll be appraised accordingly.

To be an interesting conversationalist you must be relaxed in your attitude and must display a certain modesty and open-mindedness. Do not talk dogmatically, vehemently, or belligerently in stating your opinions.

A sense of humor can be an excellent quality in conversation if you possess this precious gift, but "don't ride the horse too hard." Wit can be turned into a sharp sword to pierce the sensibilities of others.

The humorist can become so egotistical at amusing others that he transgresses the bounds of propriety and makes his classmates and the faculty the targets of his sharp arrows.

A heavy toll in broken friendships, smoldering resentments, heartfelt wounds, and injured feelings is the price exacted for uncharitable wit. Don't use the whip if you ride the horse.

To become a good conversationalist you should try to cultivate a pleasing voice; to modulate your tones; to speak with the correct volume. Never annoy your listeners with loudness or public declamation. Never embarrass other groups in a recreation room or a public place by your vociferous conversation. Regulate your voice to fit circumstances. Do these things and you will have a pleased audience. Cultivate good diction. It will help you in the pulpit.

Best Training School

There is much more that makes a good conversationalist and an attentive listener. The best method for learning these qualities is by observing oneself — and others — at recreation. If you wish to improve your conversational abilities you will find a continuous training school in the recreation room.

Just a final reminder, which shouldn't be necessary, but which embarrassing experience has made imperative: watch your grammar and your pronunciation. If you are one of those careless, slangy, recreation room expounders more intent upon a laugh than on propriety in speech, you will soon acquire grammatical blunders and barbarous pronunciations. These will betray you when you are in a cultured group.

If you think you can, magician-like, shed the harlequin jargon for the reception room conversation, you are seriously mistaken. You cannot change colors like a chameleon. So, cultivate correct grammar and proper pronunciation and you will not needlessly embarrass yourself or your brother priests in public.

Our Obligation

One last word on this subject (without sermonizing):

It is your obligation to be an exemplar in speech, not only in a negative way by avoiding profanity, but also in a positive way by using "clean speech." Vulgarity, excessive slang, stag-party repartee, off-color stories are not expected from priests. The sensibilities of the Holy Name man and those of the general public will be shocked if they hear a priest use such language.

You will administer this pledge to the Holy Name man: "I pledge myself against perjury, blasphemy, profanity, and obscene language." See that you keep it yourself, in private and in public utterances.

Do not think that you can use vulgar or profane language in the privacy of your recreation room, on the sports field, or where priests gather, or when driving a car, and then be a model of speech propriety in the parlor, or at public gatherings. Your habits will betray you.

"Speech is a mirror of the soul. As a man speaks, so is he." You wouldn't think that a pagan Roman who never had the advantages of your Christian training said that, but he did! — Publius Syrus, circa 42 B.C. Times haven't changed, in this respect, at least.

Cardinal Newman expressed it this way, in his *Idea of a University* (Discourse VII):

> The educated man is at home in any society. He has common ground with any class; he knows when to speak and when to be silent. He is able to converse, he is able to listen. He can ask a question pertinently, and gain a lesson seasonably, when he has nothing to impart himself.

Chapter 4. ANNOYING HABITS

Introspection

Most of us develop some mannerisms or eccentricities that displease or even exasperate our associates. We do not advert to these annoying traits in ourselves but we are quick to recognize them in others.

For instance, you are quick to recognize a loud, boisterous laugh in an associate but does it make you introspective? What about your own type of laughter? It may profit you to listen a bit objectively to your own laugh — and catalogue it.

Your laughter should be contagious and spontaneous but it should be controlled. If you are unfortunate enough to have a high or shrill laugh, suggesting a child's or woman's laughter, you should keep it under strict control. Nor should you indulge in the "horselaugh" or guffaw. You do not have to "shake down the rafters" in order to display your pleasure.

Some Prohibitions

There are some annoying habits that border on vulgarity. It is awkward and disconcerting even to mention them, but they are so besetting and prevalent that they cannot be ignored completely. If they do not apply to you, be duly thankful. So here goes — with them all mentioned quickly so as not to prolong a disagreeable task.

You should never, never do the following: crack knuckles; drum fingers; whistle, sing, or hum in public; vigorously scratch head (or any part of body); pick nose; sniffle; clear

throat; cough or spit obtrusively; blow nose offensively with a
trumpet effect — then examine contents of handkerchief after
using it.

Above all, you should try diligently to suppress sudden
involuntary noises such as belching and sneezing. The offense
of open sneezing is an unpardonable breach of social convention. If you can't reach your handkerchief in time, you
can always at least partially smother the germs in your hand
or clothing. Don't save your clothing at the expense of your
neighbor's comfort and health!

Other Vexations

Another disturbing practice is loud coughing in chapel
where we are in close proximity. This is particularly distract-
ing during the singing of Mass, especially to the cantors or
leaders. Such conduct on your part would merit expulsion in
a concert hall!

If you are one of those unfortunates afflicted with hay
fever, try not to remind your companions at prayer time of
your misery any more than is absolutely necessary.

And finally, there is the matter of yawning, stretching,
unnecessary movement, and shuffling of feet in chapel during
meditation, during class, or at any other assembly. If you
are tempted to indulge in any of these improprieties, just
remember how inconsiderate it is of you to disturb your
brethren at these exercises.

Careless Observance

Other social regulations concerning seminarians in regard
to which you may be inclined to become careless because of
the unusual living conditions in our seminaries and which
may carry over into normal public life, are those relative to
sitting on beds, desks, or tables, wearing hats in the house,

placing hats or overcoats on refectory tables, slamming doors, etc. Those things are prohibited by all norms of etiquette.

NOTE: There is only one way to avoid these little breaches of propriety, and that is by constant vigilance. If you catch yourself sitting on a table, get off immediately; if you become conscious that you have your hat on in the house, take it off at once. The most disturbing, however, and the most prevalent fault is slamming doors. This is particularly disconcerting during the Grand Silence, after "lights out" bell, and before rising bells. You have experienced this annoyance many times, but have you ever been an offender? Take an inventory and if you find you are a "slambanger," penalize yourself by going back and closing the door quietly. You will soon break the habit. If you fail to hold a door open for a professor who may be following you (or for that matter, a fellow student), apologize at once for your thoughtlessness. The only way you will learn to do the proper thing habitually is by constant practice until it becomes habitual. Need more be said?

One more warning: Chewing gum is for the juveniles. If you *must* chew it, do so in the privacy of your room, never in chapel, in class, nor in public. There is nothing attractive about a cleric with his jaws in constant motion. Do not resort to the lame excuse: "It is good for the breath and fine for the teeth." The answer to that is: there are commercial products on the market for these specific purposes which are much better in their results.

The sole reason for even mentioning these social aberrations here is that, like all variations from accepted forms, if they are not corrected during your formative years, they will grow into fixed habits of conduct which cannot be eradicated after you leave the seminary, or in your mature priestly life.

A Safe Guide

The reliable prescription against the above unconventional conduct is the simple one of introspection. For instance, if you note mentally the disturbing idiosyncrasies of associates, then an honest and objective examination of your own personal behavior will quickly disclose whether you are guilty of the same social fault. If so, the remedy is obvious and many of your associates will secretly thank you when they gratefully note the change.

Chapter 5. SMOKING

General

The matter of smoking is governed more by common sense than by formalized etiquette. Gone are the days when a gentleman had to ask permission to smoke in a lady's presence. Gone, too, are the days when it was considered effeminate to smoke cigarettes. Today cigars and pipes are more the exception than the rule.

Comments

Still there are a few comments worth mentioning in particular. You as a student, seminarian, or cleric, should:

a) Willingly and honestly obey the particular regulation laid down in your school, college, or seminary.

b) Manfully respect the smoking regulations as to time and place without attempting to "cut corners."

c) Restrain that impulse to reach into your pocket for the crush-proof pack when you are on the street in clerical clothes. Some people are shocked to see a clergyman smoking in public. Of course, you may consider them "squares." Take what comfort you can from St. Paul who had to write to the Corinthians, "All things are lawful for me, but not all things are expedient." So, don't smoke on the street . . . it is not expedient.

d) Keep your pipe in its rack at home, not in your coat pocket. If you are a pipe smoker, you will spare yourself much unpleasantness and some caustic thinking on the part of others if you confine your pipe smoking to your own room, the recreation room, the camp, your boating or fishing trip. The reason for this limitation is, again, that it is not expedient.

Warnings

Here are a few more comments which are worth noting:

1. The student or cleric should not have nicotine-stained fingers. Such stains will be an offense to some of the people to whom you will ultimately minister. The prospective priest who thinks this discoloration is not offensive to others is not thinking properly.

2. If you are one of those clerics who must have a cigarette immediately upon rising, or one of those who must have a "few drags" between classes or exercises, just advert to the conclusion that you are becoming addicted to a demanding habit.

3. From a slightly different approach, the observation may be made that odors are important in forming impressions. The cigarette or cigar breath (not to mention pipe) is repugnant to many people.

4. And remember, later on you will serve some people who will not like to receive Holy Communion from you if you have tobacco odor clinging to your fingers from that before Mass smoke.

5. Along the same line of thought, the odor of stale cigarette, cigar, or pipe smoke will permeate your clothing. You may not be conscious of this "fragrance" which your garments exude, but your close neighbor may be disagreeably affected by it. Of course, if smoking is not permitted *indoors* at your seminary this caution is unnecessary.

6. When, however, you smoke *outdoors* on the seminary grounds, don't litter the walks with butts. A good expedient

here is the old Army one, of disposing of butts by tearing the paper, spreading the tobacco and rolling up the paper into a small wad. It helps greatly in policing grounds.

Prohibitions

Here are a few warnings given by an authority on this subject (*New Esquire Etiquette*):

1. Don't smoke in full view of a three-foot sign saying "No Smoking." You may get away with it until the stewardess reproves you or the guard spots you. But those few quick drags will cause raised eyebrows and questioning looks in your immediate periphery. And if you have to be reprimanded, the scene could conceivably result in much embarrassment to you or to your traveling companions. You don't want them to explode with the gasoline or oxygen tank!

2. It is best not to smoke in crowds — crowded elevators, parade crushes, pushing lines of people, but this is, of course, a matter of safety. There is no convincing way to say "I'm sorry" as you watch your neighbor go up in smoke.

3. No less binding are the unwritten "No Smoking" signs you encounter in private homes. Even nonsmoking hostesses, unless they are violent objectors, usually offer cigarettes or at least provide ashtrays. But now and then you'll run into a place absolutely barren of smoking accessories. That's your tip-off — you'd better lay off the weed for the nonce. Give up as graciously as you can. Next time you can stay home.

4. At the table of gourmets or of conservative and formal hosts, you are *not* welcome to smoke during the dinner. Let the table setting be your guide. If there are cigarettes and ashtrays at your place, feel free to light up whenever you like. If not, wait until cigarettes are passed or until the dinner is over. Even if the makings are in full view, think twice before smoking between courses among people who carefully

savor their food. It is a demonstrable fact that smoke dulls the palate, and the mere odor of your cigarette will interfere with others' enjoyment of the food. This admonition also applies when you are in a dining car, restaurant, or other public eating place, especially if you are seated with strangers.

5. When visiting, whether the cigarette is your host's or your own, it should be managed with respect for property. Ashes may indeed be "good for the rug" but let your hostess do her own spreading. Never put a cigarette down on the edge of a piece of furniture, even if you're positive you'll remember to pick it up before it scars the surface. And don't take it for granted that every candy dish and lamp base is intended as an ashtray, either. You may always ask for an ashtray if none is available, and you may always ask to be checked on what is and is not an ashtray. You may be sure that food dishes, coasters, empty fireplaces, vases and growing plants are *not*.

Importunity

Try to smoke attractively. Even if you are wearing a cassock (or a black rabat) there's no excuse for letting ashes sprinkle down your front. Almost any mannerism which makes the cigarette an attached part of you is equally unbecoming; the cigarette dangling from your mouth while you talk, or shake hands, or tip your hat . . . the cloud of smoke which obscures you to the person who is talking to you . . . the odd bits of tobacco or paper which cling to your teeth, your chin, or lips . . . all these are in poor form. So try to smoke attractively. You may not succeed, but you can get an "A" for effort.

Chapter 6. TABLE MANNERS

Introduction

Your manners at table will be the ultimate criterion by which you will be judged by others. Your conformity to accepted standards of proper table behavior will become the norm for appraisal of your entire social "culture."

Expressed a bit differently, your table manners will indicate very decidedly what kind of seminarian you are.

Here is one set of circumstances where you cannot plead "ignorance of the law." You are simply supposed to know and to observe the proper amenities. No other single social usage provides such a pragmatical appraisal of you as the way you eat. This is evidenced from the amount of space given by authorities in their books on etiquette to this phase of social conduct.

This chapter will enumerate some general observations which will apply to you as a seminarian — at table.

These comments will not be all-inclusive, for the table arrangement, the seating, the serving, the silent meal with reading, or the conversation-at-table — all these differ for the various seminaries and their established customs. Hence, these observations have different degrees of application to your specific circumstances. You will have to adapt them to your particular conditions, but most of them will have general application.

The cautions and warnings, however, do affect you personally, irrespective of the special eating arrangements in your seminary.

Cautions

If you are a preparatory student residing at home and eating at the family table you cannot (and should not) attempt to force seminary table manners on your family. It will suffice for you to know how to conduct yourself properly at the home table — and to practice your knowledge as much as possible — with reasonable consideration for the rest of your family.

A few examples will illustrate the necessity for this policy. In this chapter and the following one you will learn (if you do not already know) that you do not break saltines into your soup; do not prop your knife and fork between the rim of your dinner plate and the table cloth; do not butter a whole slice of bread at one time; do not pick up your asparagus in your fingers and imitate a sword swallower.

You must practice these regulations regularly and faithfully, irrespective of what other members of your family do in this regard. The reason for this is simple: you become almost a slave to habit. If you are accustomed to committing any one of these social faults at home, your habitual conduct will expose you to critical appraisal when you dine elsewhere than at the family table.

In other words, your particular training should not be neglected until you seat yourself in the major seminary refectory. Your family life and your junior schooling should include your social culture as well as your scholastic accomplishments.

You should not, however, set yourself up as a paragon and make a nuisance of yourself by burdening your family with your ostentatious display.

It will suffice for you to learn and to observe the rules yourself. You need not broadcast your knowledge and punctilious conformity to the other members of the family. You will only visibly embarrass them and disclose your own self-centered traits. Don't be prissy!

Later on the same caution will apply when you receive your first assignment as an assistant priest. You, fresh from the seminary, will be keenly aware of your correct table etiquette and of your proper observance of it. But (and here is the caution) don't try to reform your venerable pastor's table manners — either by gentle hint, or by ostentatious display of your observance.

Mentally note this fact — and accept it realistically — that no matter how fanatical or zealous you are on this subject of table manners, you are not going to change the pastor's table "rubrics" any more than you are his set way of celebrating Mass and delivering sermons.

This table experience may be the first real opportunity you have had for the practical application of that charity, and fraternal love mentioned in the Introduction to this book, and which you have been studying theoretically for so many years — so don't miss it!

Be humble enough to realize that the pastor will have ample and just criticism of your incompetence and inexperience in practical parish matters without your adding "fuel to the fire" by subtle censorship of his possible table unconventionality.

In practice it will be sufficient for you to be resolute and quietly consistent in your table proprieties without attracting attention by your strained observance of them. You will not reform the pastor (and again, don't try). But you would be startled to know that the pastor will secretly admire the culture of his new assistant and publicly boast of "my fine young assistant" to his fraternal peers. Now some other warnings.

Warnings

In some minor seminaries and in some major ones there may be deviations from standard practices. But these exceptions are not a flaunting of the social regulations. They are necessitated by sheer utility or by special circumstances.

For instance, the normal table settings of plates and silverware, butter plates, dessert spoons, etc., may not be observed in your particular seminary. The reason for this is that the institution simply does not have (and probably cannot afford) the necessary man power to provide this specialized service.

But you, as an observant student, will note these peculiarities as exemptions from the accepted forms. This advertence will prepare you to follow the normal procedures in table manners elsewhere under conventional regulations. If you know the correct usage these variations will not confuse you when you meet normal situations.

With this preamble, here are some special comments for you, the prospective priest.

General Observations

It is easy for you to acquire poor table manners in the seminary during your secluded years of study, but it is very difficult for you to overcome them in your active service years.

Poor table manners can be a real detriment to your priestly ministry and they can cause acute embarrassment to your host and hostess when you display them in private homes or in other rectories.

If you exercise ordinary care during your years of study, your correct table manners will, to a large extent, become habitual or second nature.

For instance, later on when you, the priest, are invited to

a public banquet or to a private home, you will have neither the time, nor the opportunity to advert to proper table manners or to watch how other guests conduct themselves.

The conversation at the table will so preoccupy your attention and you will have to become such an active participant in it, that there will be no time for concentration on correct table etiquette; hence, it must be ingrained in your formative years so that it becomes almost automatic in its subsequent use.

Some Useful Refreshers

It is a normal assumption by your superiors that you possess at least the rudiments of proper table manners when you enter the seminary. The following admonishments are intended as a quick refresher course in what you already know; a brief stressing of specific minutiae.

1. The proper seated position for you at table is comfortably *erect;* not slouching or slumping.

2. Your best position for your feet is with both firmly on the floor. Resist the temptation to extend the legs full length in a straight line.

Your feet *may be* crossed at the ankles, but never at the knees; nor should they be entwined around the rungs of the chair.

This entwining habit may betray you when you are dining out and cause your hostess some apprehension as to the finish on her dining room chairs.

The safe and sure method is for you to become accustomed to sitting with both feet firmly on the floor. This habitual practice will be insurance against embarrassment when you are "company."

Some other "pitfalls" you may need to be reminded of are:

bending your head to meet the food; using your elbows as pivots to convey food to your mouth, or failing to pass dishes. Others will be mentioned in their proper place.

Consideration of Others

One of your distinguishing marks as a gentlemanly seminarian will be your consideration of your confreres at table. You in effect will play host to them without fanfaronade or display. You will always be alert to their needs.

For instance, if you do not wish a service from a dish in front of you, bread for example, you will not ignore the dish, but promptly pass it on to your neighbor who may be waiting for that particular item.

You will be considerate of your adjacent diners. Never "stock up" on bread, cookies, fruit, etc., which are passed to you from a common dish. More supplies will be furnished later on during the meal, and if not, then you have an excellent opportunity to exercise virtue.

Show some consideration for your neighbor if the variety of bread, cookies, etc., is limited when the dish reaches you. Do not take *all* the pieces of one variety and leave him no choice. Limit your selection until another opportunity presents itself for you to secure additional pieces of your preference.

If somebody at the table, below or above you, has signaled for a second helping of bread, or any dish, do not interrupt its course of passage in order to help yourself to an additional serving. Wait until the first applicant has been served, then have the dish passed back to you.

If there is a limited amount of food on the common dish when it reaches you and there are others to be served from this same quantity, gauge your helping accordingly. Do not "hog" the favorite delicacy.

The Left-Handed

If you are left-handed do not rearrange the table setting. Learn to use your cup and saucer, your water glass, your salad dish, your bread and butter plate in the right-hand setting. How you use your knife, fork, and silverware in right or left hand is immaterial. But you cannot change the table arrangement when you dine out, so become accustomed to the normal setting at home.

Some Pertinent Points

Be careful of the linens, particularly the table cloth. In some seminaries plastic covers are used over the linen table-cloths — a practice which engenders carelessness. Beware of indifference in this regard.

The napkin (dinner-size in most houses) is placed on your lap opened in half. Its purpose is to wipe the lips and finger-tips. It is never used as a towel to dry your face, or tucked in as a bib to protect your clothing. At the end of the meal you return the napkin neatly folded to the napkin ring.

Ordinarily, guest napkins are used only for the one meal. In such cases the guest casually leaves the napkin partially folded on the table. If guests are to remain for several meals, they are supplied with guest napkin rings.

Do not acquire that habit of "polishing" the silverware on the napkin before the start of the meal. If the silverware is not clean, quietly indicate to the server to bring you a clean piece.

If you are supplied (as may happen in your seminary) with only one knife, fork, and spoon, you must adjust your strategy to meet this emergency. Just remember that the silverware, once used, is never returned to the table cloth, but remains flat on the plate or dish.

Knives and forks are never propped on the side of the plate. Nothing will betray your lack of social grace so pointedly as balancing knife or fork on the side of the plate. It is an affront to any hostess.

Place your knife or fork flat on the plate but toward the side when not in use. Place them firmly on the plate with the knife edge turned in when finished.

Here we come to the T-shirt again. Do not push up or roll up the sleeves of the cassock to expose the bare arms. The cassock ordinarily will be worn all your priestly life at meals, so you may as well learn to adjust to it in the beginning.

Begin eating as soon as you are served, if that is the custom in your seminary. Otherwise observe your special regulations. Eat at a moderate pace; do not bolt your food, nor dawdle over it.

Chew silently and with the mouth closed. Nature has provided the lips with sufficient flexibility, so that they need not be parted in masticating food.

Conclusion

These detailed warnings may seem to you to be superfluous, but practical experience has fully demonstrated the necessity for mentioning them specifically.

In fact, prepare yourself for more appalling details in the next chapter.

Chapter 7. THE CONVENTIONALITY OF EATING

Source Material

Authority for this chapter is the book *New Esquire Etiquette For Men* (Lippincott, 1959). The section on Table Manners is reproduced here with the gracious consent of the editors. The chapter has been condensed somewhat in this reproduction, and some comments added, but the matter and the form are that of the original text. The style may appear to some rather flippant and negative, but beneath the light approach is positive common sense advice about correct table manners. This chapter can be read for laughs, but the thoughtful seminarian will read it with discernment and introspection.

Table Manners

When eating, the idea is to do it neatly, quietly, and all but incidentally. If anything bothers you about table manners, put the question to these three tests. If the technique (1) makes a mess, (2) makes a noise, (3) calls attention to the fact that you are determined to stuff yourself, it's bad manners.

A fourth general "don't" assumes equal importance: don't be prissy. Don't cock your little finger or pat-pat your pursed mouth daintily with your napkin.

The way you eat is a matter of habit. If your unconscious eating habits are unattractive even your best friend (or closest classmate) won't tell you.

But *you* can tell; watch yourself for these signs of the four scourges of the dining table. But also read carefully for the correct eating habits.

Here art the four scourges: (1) the Slob; (2) the Racketeer; (3) the Pig; (4) the Priss. Each will be described in detail.

Four Horrible Examples

I. The Slob

He ties his napkin around his neck or tucks it into his vest. The napkin belongs on your lap during a meal, as stated in the preceding chapter.

Do not permit overseas students or pretentious epicureans to impress you by citing how the napkin is used in London, Paris, and Rome. The simple and inflexible rule for you in the U. S. A. is the napkin on your lap!

He leaves a sample of every course on the rim of his drinking glass. He sins on two counts; he drinks when his mouth is not empty, and he neglects to use his napkin before using the glass.

He makes every mouthful a full course meal in miniature (and not so miniature at that). Instead, of course, he should take small bites, chewing and swallowing each bite before he takes the next.

He should keep separate foods separate on his plate, if that's the way they were intended. Sauces and gravies may be poured directly onto the food for which they were intended, but jellies, condiments, and all other accessories should be put on the plate in virgin state, only then to be spread on the bread or forked onto meat in bite-sized portions.

He forms a bridge from table to plate with his knife and fork when they are not in use — with handles on cloth, working ends propped on plate. Beware of this fault! As stated before (in the preceding chapter) nothing will betray your lack of social grace so quickly as this *faux pas*. Place your knife and fork flat on the plate when they are not on active duty.

He spits out anything he doesn't like. (You don't have to eat the inedible, of course, and if you *must* remove something from your mouth, first be sure that it bears no resemblance to regurgitated food, then grasp and remove it with your fingers — that's the quickest way. Correctly you could take it out with the same spoon or fork it went in on, but this maneuver is too acrobatic for grace in most instances, and it runs dangerously close to spitting. Actually you can cut out bones and stones before they get into your mouth. And you can manfully swallow something that offends your palate.)

He breaks saltines into his soup! As a rule if a cracker is meant to go into the soup, it is meant to go in whole. But put oyster crackers first on your butter plate or on the cloth, then drop them into your soup, whole, a few at a time. Croutons are spooned directly into the soup. Saltines are placed on your butter plate and are munched between spoonfuls of soup.

Remember, never break saltines into the soup. No other table fault will catalogue your cultural status quicker than this one breach of convention. If you have already acquired this gauche trait "break it" at once before it "turns state evidence" on you!

He eats messy things with his fingers. The best way to decide when to pick food up with your fingers is to decide *in advance* whether you can do it neatly. Picnics are something else again, of course, and some foods like lobsters are messy whatever your *modus operandi,* but with neatness as your guide you can't go far wrong. This neatness guide works both ways: it's neater to pick up an ear of corn than to watch it skitter across the plate as you try to cut it; it is neater to leave the hard stalk of asparagus if you can't cut it with a fork as you did the tips. And if an approach by hand seems indicated, as with a sandwich or a piece of fresh fruit, it is neater to cut it into manageable sections before you pick it up.

He puts soiled silver on the table. He spoons coffee from cup into mouth, or leaves the spoon in the cup. He does the dishwashing or silver polishing at the table. If the implement is really not clean, ignore it as you would a hair in your soup. (In a restaurant, of course, you may ask for another fork or send the soup back.)

He puts his mouth into the food instead of the food into his mouth. You shouldn't meet your food even halfway. You bring it up to your erect head; you don't duck down to meet it coming up. He shoves spaghetti into his mouth with loose ends dangling instead of rolling it on his fork.

He talks with his mouth full; gesticulates and points with his eating tools; blows on his food, instead of waiting quietly for it to cool enough to eat; he dunks his toast or rolls into his coffee.

He cleans his teeth at table — with toothpick or finger-nail; by sucking at them or by running his tongue around his teeth, with grimaces.

II. The Racket-eer

He chews with his mouth open, making no attempt to muffle the noise (or conceal the sight) of his cement-mixer mastication. He clanks silver on silver, or silver on plate.

He stirs his coffee fiendishly, like a witch standing over a boiling cauldron, and every revolution of the spoon sets up a racket. When he puts his knife and fork down, you wonder that the force does not smash the plate. He winds up by scraping his plate with his fork. And if he's the "helpful" as well as the noisy type, his final sin against the eardrums is to stack his dishes, crashingly.

He slurps his soup. Suction is superfluous — just put the side of the spoon in your mouth and sip quietly.

He drums on the table, or cracks his knuckles, or chews on the ice from his water glass, or otherwise sounds off between noisy bites.

He pushes away from the table at dinner's end, with both hands shoving against the table edge and the chair screeching across the floor. Instead you should reach down and lift the chair back as you rise slightly.

III. The Pig

He digs in the moment he is served. He knows he doesn't have to wait for the hostess, who will be served last, but he's apparently too hungry to remember that he should wait until two or three others at the table have also been served. (This practice applies when you are a guest at another's table. When you are in your own seminary you follow the custom of your house, as mentioned in the previous chapter.)

He uses a piece of bread, tightly gripped in his hand, to mop up every last drop of sauce, every last morsel of food. His plate then looks as if it had just come out of the dishwasher. If his favorite food is bread and gravy, he may break off a small piece of bread, drop it into the sauce, then eat the bread with his fork — but he shouldn't scrub or mop or use an unbroken slice of bread.

He spreads butter on his bread in midair and all at once, as if he intended to eat the whole piece in one bite. Except in the case of tiny, hot biscuits, bread should be broken and buttered only as needed — in quarters or bite sizes. It should be held against the rim of the butter plate during the spreading, and not waved all over the place or held chest high.

He cuts up his whole plateful of food at one time, as if he couldn't bear to stop eating once he had begun. Unless he is under ten years old (and we are not) he should cut his food only as he eats it.

He drinks his coffee and spoons his soup with a loud sucking noise. He tilts his soup bowl or plate toward him. Properly, he would tip it away from him, just as — properly — he would spoon the soup away from him. But this is not the shortest distance between two points, and the pig is blatantly starving.

He elbows his way through the meal. When he cuts, his elbows are like flapping wings. When he eats, his spare arm serves as a prop, enabling him to eat much faster. Elbows on the table are "socially acceptable" when you are not eating, but the safest course is to keep your spare hand in your lap. While you're eating, your elbows should be as close to your body as in a good golf swing.

He gnaws on bones, as if he's afraid to miss the tiniest morsel of meat.

He sucks his fingers, on the same sort of compulsion. If he is so messy as to get food on his fingers, he should use a finger bowl and/or the napkin, not his lips, to clean up.

He squeezes the last drop of juice from his half grapefruit. If you can't get it out with a spoon it's out of bounds.

Finally, when he's finished he pushes his plate away from him as if to say, "Well, *that* was good, *now* what do we eat?" Instead, he should sit quietly without rearranging the table, without pushing or tilting his chair back, and without loosening his belt.

IV. The Priss

He purses his lips when he eats — in exaggerated "refinement." He couldn't look less pleased if he were eating cyanide or castor oil.

He leaves a little of everything on his plate, in terror of appearing greedy. What a waste! If he doesn't intend to eat it, he shouldn't take it.

He daintily curves his little finger when using his cup — an affected gesture of "grace." His stagecraft is a "dead giveaway" of his interior motivation.

He is always saying that he doesn't like or "can't eat" certain foods. If he is not blessed with a catholic taste, or a genuine enjoyment of all foods strange and familiar, he should *pretend* that he is. The very least he can do is keep quiet about his allergies and his prejudices.

He is a hesitant, obvious copycat, making everybody else as nervous as he over which fork to use. *It is not that important!* If you can do it unobtrusively, it is all very well to watch your hostess or more knowledgeable guests to see how they handle certain unfamiliar dishes. But if your concentration on the fine points of etiquette is going to make you an inattentive conversationalist, shrug off your worries. It might help you to know that silver is placed on the table in the order of its use, the fork farthest from your plate, on the outside, being meant for the first fork food, the one on the inside for the last. If you are served both fork and spoon for dessert you may use both (spoon for the ice cream, say, and fork for the meringue), or you may use the fork to hold the dessert steady while you cut and eat it with the spoon, or you may simply use whichever seems more appropriate. The butter plate and glasses on your *right* are for you; your salad, unless served as a separate course, is on your *left*. But no one worth knowing will care if you use a fork when a spoon was intended, and if you don't get flustered and apologetic, no one will even notice.

He is afraid to use a knife on his salad because he's heard it's not proper. If there is a salad knife at his place, he can be sure that it is not only proper but expected. And if he can't manage the salad neatly with his fork alone, it's better to use his dinner knife than to emulate a rabbit, with lettuce hanging out of his mouth.

He transfers his fork from left hand to right after he has cut his meat, even though it is more natural for him to eat with tines-down fork in his left hand. *Either* way of eating is "correct." So whether you learned to eat by the Continental or the crisscross method there's no point in changing your style to fit whatever the current fashion happens to be.

In Retrospect

The comments and regulations in this and the preceding chapter on table manners cover the normal situations that may arise in the seminary refectory. You will not remember all of them by one reading any better than you will master the rubrics for the subdeacon in one session.

If you are convinced of the importance of good table manners you will do the same thing as you do with your sacristy rituals — you will read this guidebook over and over; you will consult it when in doubt; you will be so familiar with its contents that good table manners become second nature, force of habit, to you.

Chapter 8. WAITING ON TABLE

General

One of your important duties as a seminarian is waiting on table. This task will offer you an excellent opportunity to develop your character and to practice virtue.

The task is not a menial one. It is a practical application of the classroom principles of the love of God and the love of neighbor. It is a "Martha" service to God; it is a fraternal ministration to faculty or fellow seminarian.

Your mental approach to the assignment and your attitude toward the discharge of this duty can create an atmosphere of sunshine or one of gloom. It can affect not only you but also those you serve.

Your mental disposition should not be that of a reluctant recruit assigned to K.P. duty, but rather that of a willing volunteer in the uniform of Christ, eager to be helpful.

You are not a professional waiter expecting a generous tip for fawning service. You are a seminarian, a man of God, pleasantly discharging your duty as a part of your ministry. This attitude will carry over into the services you render as a priest and make them a labor of love.

This frame of mind, strangely enough, will make your assignment all the more agreeable to you, and also to those you wait on. They will be more at ease and less formal or rigid if you, the waiter, let them realize it is your pleasure to serve them.

There are several factors which will help you to be an efficient waiter and an amiable attendant.

44

Personal Appearance

Personal appearance is very important, for your own internal confidence and for the impression you create in those to whom you minister.

You should be well groomed: your shoes shined, trousers creased, hair brushed, hands and fingernails clean, shirt immaculate. If at all possible long sleeved shirts should be worn. It isn't particularly conducive to a faculty member's appetite to view a hairy, brawny, bare arm placing the food before him. If you wear a white coat or apron, it should be spotless, pressed, and properly and neatly arranged on your person.

Consideration

Your manner of serving and your mental attitude toward your duty definitely create a magnetic field, a radar system, which alerts the diner and which can materially affect his entire meal.

For instance, if you are overly formal and precise in your bearing, or conversely, if you are indifferent and apathetic in your manner you can be sure you will not establish a harmonious bond with those you serve.

You must be interested and responsive to your work, attentive to your duties, and quick to anticipate the diner's desires or needs.

Attentive

If you are a thoughtful waiter you will be attentive and alert to details. You will make a mental inventory of the table setting to determine if everything is accounted for and in the proper place. You will be attentive to guests or visitors to see that they are provided with napkins and complete accessories.

You will be prepared to meet any emergency, such as spilled coffee, overturned dish, dropped silverware, etc. You will remedy the situation quietly and effectively with the least possible embarrassment to all concerned.

Service for Faculty

The stewards or supervisors of the refectory have already instructed you and your classmates in the customs and manner of serving the faculty members in your particular seminary under your established conditions.

1. The following is merely a "refresher" course.
   a) Serve all food from the left.
   b) Remove dishes from the right.
   c) Pour all beverages from the right. Take the cup and saucer (or glass) in your hand, stand back from the table and pour; then return the receptacle to the table with care.

NOTE: This method is obviously hazardous. It is more practical to pour liquids while the cup or glass remains stationary on the table. Only in the case where the seating arrangement prevents this method is the cup or glass lifted from the table.

In that case, take the cup and saucer in your own hand to do the pouring and give it back carefully to the diner. In no case should you permit the diner to hold the cup and saucer while you pour. This may result in complete disaster — scalded thumb, crashing china, and spilt beverage.

In any event, whatever practice is customary in your seminary, you should take care not to spill the contents on the person, table, or saucer. Be prepared for these risks and if an accident occurs remedy it as quickly as possible.

Use an extra napkin to absorb as much of the liquid as possible. Replace the saucer with a clean one, or if none is available dry the saucer. If the liquid was spilt on the table-cloth, spread an extra napkin over the spot and apologize.

2. The sequence of the courses is: first, appetizer, then the salad, then the main course.

The main course always follows a set pattern of serving: first the meat, then the potatoes, then the other vegetables. (The order is easy to remember from the sequence in the alphabet M-P-V.)

3. When the priest has finished, remove the dishes quietly and serve the dessert and coffee. Make sure the priest has the proper silverware for these items. Be careful not to rush the priest, yet don't be so slow as to appear negligent.

Some priests may desire their coffee (or tea) with the main course. If so, readily oblige them, then offer them more with the dessert.

4. Be attentive. See that the priests' water glasses are kept filled. Don't make them ask you for more beverage or for additional butter or bread. Anticipate their needs! Keep everything hot!

5. In seeking to determine a priest's particular wishes regarding food or drink, or in determining if he is finished, you must not startle him from behind his chair by a question unexpectedly spoken into his ear. First approach the priest so that he becomes conscious of your presence; ask your question once you have gained his attention.

6. Always travel behind the table. The priests may not mention it, but it is annoying to them for a waiter to constantly cross in front of the table when going from side to side. Stay back of their backs!

7. Remove dishes from the table quietly. Do not clank the dishes together, nor stack them noisily. Don't be a "racket-eer" waiter.

8. Do not open up a chatty conversation with the priests.

If they address you answer them respectfully, but do not make this an opportunity for prolonging the conversation.

9. Be pleasant under all circumstances and under all provocations. Cheerfulness is contagious. Remember if Father wasn't pleased with the food he at least had a pleasant waiter!

Summary

If the foregoing simple procedures are kept in mind you will do much to make the meal more enjoyable for the priests.

By your cheerful attitude and your agreeable manner you may perhaps unconsciously be establishing a fine tradition of service in your seminary. You may some day be a faculty member at that very table and reap the harvest you helped to sow!

If that time does come (when you are a faculty member) you will find yourself judging the character of the seminarian who waits on you by the same standards by which you were judged when you performed similar service. You will find then that the manner in which a seminarian waits on your table will afford you a fine objective method of character analysis. In this duty the seminarian will unconsciously display his temperament, disposition, spirit, resourcefulness, humor, cooperation and individuality in his every movement. So reflect on your attitude now. It may help you greatly in the future!

Service for Students

What has already been covered applies with equal force to you who wait on the students. There is less formality, of course, but the same alertness and efficiency is expected of the waiters. Here are some admonitions.

1. One hindrance to efficiency could be prolonged conversation among the waiters or with a student being served.

Save the classroom and athletic field postmortems for the recreation period.

2. Be alert to your duties. You should know what is expected of you and you should anticipate situations, especially emergencies.

3. Avoid clumsiness with concentration and confidence. Learn your job of waiting as you would any other task. Your mental attitude, as mentioned before, could be responsible for your ineptness.

4. Be obliging and patient with the students. The waiter's temperament has a definite effect, for better or worse, on those at the table.

5. Do not hurry the students at their meal by removing the dishes too quickly. Allow a reasonable time for the slow eaters and for those who relish their food.

6. Set an example of fraternal teamwork and cooperation by sharing any extra duties and assisting in emergencies caused by accidents, so that no one waiter may be overburdened while you stand by nonchalantly.

Students' Cooperation

The students being served by their fellow seminarians also have their obligations, such as

1. Be helpful and considerate of the waiter. He is not a "hired hand," but a fellow student performing his assigned duty.

2. Be reasonable in your requests of the waiter. He has his limitations and he has others to serve.

3. Do not hesitate to *request* but never *demand* service from the waiter.

4. Always keep in mind that soon the situation may be reversed and you may be the waiter. Do unto the waiter as you would have him do unto you when you serve.

Chapter 9. TIPPING

General

Let's face it: Tipping is here to stay. No matter what your personal feelings (or attitude) may be about tipping, *you* will not change the system. It's been with us a long time and it's "still going strong." The only practical result you will achieve by a reformist attitude is to lose face for yourself and indirectly for your clerical fraternity.

Rugged individualism in this matter will accomplish nothing except dark looks and mumbling undertones. Oh, yes, one thing more: a retentive memory by the waiter or barber, or any service man when you do a repeat performance.

So contain yourself for there is no moral issue involved. Put a padlock on your lofty principles, remove it from your pocketbook, and resign yourself to the system. No matter how you fight back you can't win, so don't drag your heels in this matter or cause visible embarrassment to your guests.

Moreover, and this is the clincher: You, the seminarian (or the priest), are expected to be a generous tipper. How this conclusion was reached is immaterial — it is a working fact in social situations. So you will impair the dignity of the clerical state if you show yourself parsimonious or "against" the system.

Yet, on the other hand, you must not be so liberal in your tips as to give the impression that priests abound in wealth. There is a theological principle which is a good guide in this matter: "In medio stat virtus." Don't swing to either extreme.

In our day and age tips have become fairly well standard-
ized, at least there is a low and a high ceiling — a flexible
range in which you can operate with mental (and financial)
poise. Just where you calibrate on this scale will be determined by your technique and your latitude. But, again, don't
jeopardize the par value of the clergy stock in this market.

Some Valuable "Tips"

Don't overtip ostentatiously; you embarrass your guests and
even the waiter — not by the amount but by the showmanship.

The proper way to tip is for you to do it privately and
quietly, but graciously, even if it hurts you. Look the waiter
in the eye with a smile and say "Thank you" as if you meant
it — which you should.

If the service performed for you (whether in the dining
room or elsewhere) is "beyond the call of duty" you may
show your appreciation by a larger tip than is normal, but
do it without ceremony, yet with sincerity.

In reverse: Don't undertip. You save money but you lose
face. Even if the service you received is not up to standard,
the least you can tip is the minimum-norm, the low ceiling.
This is the only way you can register your disapproval of the
service — by withholding the *extra* tip you would have given
for efficient and pleasant service.

Comment: And here is a gratuitous tip for you: Don't
complain publicly about the service to the waiter or to the
one who renders the service to you. It will accomplish nothing
tangible. The deed is done. Your complaint will not remedy
matters.

You will only attract unfavorable attention to your party
and embarrass your companions especially the ladies, if they
are present.

If you have a justifiable major complaint about the food

or the service, take the matter up with the management —
and do it quietly and with self-control.

The most effective method of registering your displeasure
is the withholding of your patronage — you don't have to go
back to that particular establishment.

(This comment is an "interlude" . . . now back to the tips.)

One more don't: You know that some tips are subtle
extortion, but don't try to reform the "racket." The quarter
you give the hatcheck girl, you know she doesn't get a cent
of it; the money you give the boy who "watches your car" at
a sport's event, you know he doesn't put an eye on it.

But these and many other crafty. "pulls upon the purse"
must be borne with silent resignation. If you don't conform
you are termed a "tightwad" or a "hick." Maybe the label
won't bother you much, but it will be extended to include all
the members of the cloth — and you don't want to be responsible for that development.

If you are in doubt whether a tip will be expected or re-
jected, offer the tip as if you were asking a favor. The rule
here was laid down by a serviceman: "The only reason anyone is ever 'insulted' by a tip is because it's not up to their
standard of what a tip should be."

The price of tipping, like all prices, is going up as the
purchasing power of money declines. For example, the pastor
used to give the little boy a penny for running to the corner
for the evening sports edition of the paper, now it costs you
a nickel. The shoeshine boy gets a ten-cent tip today where
in times past that was the cost of the service itself.

So resign yourself to the inevitable, for the size of tips is
spiraling with the cost of living. The movement of prices has
always been upward and there is no economic or social reason
to predict that it will reverse itself. A rough and a safe guide

today for most situations you will meet in your regular routine is a 15 to 20 percent tip on the total of the charge.

A situation may arise where you have received exceptional service, or when you may have asked for some special attention. In either case the tip may be increased proportionately to your appreciation, yet it should never suggest the lavish or reckless spender. Waiters and other employees have a nicely balanced sense of fitness. You may pamper it but don't distort it.

Practical Application

There is no necessity of detailing here the scale of tipping situations you will meet when you leave the seminary and enter upon your normal priestly life. You probably won't remember them for that length of time, and by then the scale may have climbed to aerial heights — today's values will probably be obsolete by then.

However, if you are speculatively interested in present-day standards you will find them compiled in the *New Esquire Etiquette for Men,* which should be available in your library, certainly in the public library. Just look up the Index under "Tipping." It covers the normal situations you will meet, as well as the unusual, at clubs, golf courses, weekends, and many other situations.

If you have ambitions for foreign study there is a special section in that book for the system in effect abroad, on the continent and elsewhere, on the ocean liner that takes you across, and the many outstretched hands you will encounter when you get through customs. These gratuities differ radically in many cases from our local customs. The important warning here is *do not* use your own U. S. scale of tipping (or trust your own judgment) in foreign situations. Consult your host, or experienced traveling companion, or other foreign authority, when you are confronted with this different situation of values. You may save yourself and the members of your group much embarrassment (and loss of face) by ascertaining exactly what is expected of you under given circumstances.

Mention may be made here, however, of one situation you may encounter during your student days, namely, taxicabs.

Taxicabs

The minimum amount you give a taxi driver is 50 cents, even for taking you around the corner.

The normal scale for metered service today is about a 20 or 25 cent tip for each $1 ride.

If the driver gets out of his cab to lift your bags or give some other extra service, your thanks may be shown in a larger tip. Or if he has waited for you over a few minutes without meter running, you may indicate your appreciation in your tip.

No Show: If you telephone for a cab and then change your mind, you are required in all fairness to reimburse the driver when he arrives for the "no show." He has spent his time and mileage in coming to your address. Moreover, if you fail to pay for the "no show" you jeopardize the seminary's reputation (or the rectory's) with the cab companies and future calls from the same address may have difficulty getting prompt service. An amount of 50 cents is about right.

NOTE: This "no show" carries over into air and train reservations. If, for instance, you have an airplane reservation and the weather becomes threatening and you decide to take the train, you are in all fairness obligated to cancel the unused space, so that it may be available for some "standby" who desires occupancy but can't get it unless you release your reserved space. At present the air lines are charging a percentage of the fare, from five to forty percent, in fact, for "no show." So keep this in mind too.

Credit Cards

Travelers, today, carry little cash but many Credit Cards and Travelers Checks. You can charge your gasoline, your flight fare, your railroad expense. You can sign for your motel, "say it with flowers," or send gifts.

In the dining room no money changes hands. You can dine, wine, and tip without cash. You sign for the meal and write in the amount of the tip for the waiter.

This, for the present, is a purely academic supposition for you, the seminarian. It will, however, become practical when you have acquired more maturity and rank, more girth and bank balance.

Then a psychological phenomenon will take place. The added prestige of "signing for it" instead of "paying now" will lift you out of the normal 15 to 20 percent tipping class and you will pencil in a tip in the 25 to 30 percent bracket. It will be painless.

The reaction will set in later on — when you receive the statement for your splurge and get out your checkbook. Maybe it was worth it!

Chapter 10. SPORTS

Introduction

You can put it down as axiomatic: In all sports, indoor and outdoor, the American boy of all ages (and the seminarian minor or major) is out to win. This "win" urge carries over into adult sports, whether it is cards or chess, bowling or boating.

You meet this competitive spirit at all levels from the grade school boy to the professional athlete. And for each sport there is one elemental *unwritten* law of sport conduct: "Ignorance of the rules is no excuse."

For instance, anything that looks like cheating, or has the appearance of sharp practice, according to the code (even though you are inexperienced with the behavior pattern) will change your reputation from "First Class" to "Poor Sport."

The punishment for your violation of this unexpressed code will be immediate and irrevocable: You will be labeled as a "wrong guy." You can never live it down; there is no court of appeal from this verdict. No extenuating circumstances; no beginner's mistake; no error of judgment may be pleaded — the verdict is final. The reasoning is simple: "You are supposed to know the code before you play."

The Rigid Test

Even you, the seminarian, when you play away from your own campus, will not escape this irrevocable judgment, if you break the code of the game, either through naïveté or ignorance. And your friend, or sponsor, at the club or park, will not defend you, or excuse you. He will only be visibly embarrassed that you have violated an unwritten law. You will be in the "doghouse" for keeps; you will be a "wrong guy" with that group. You will not be welcomed to their circle a second time. So the moral here is: Learn the rules and observe the code before you play. You can't make "honest" mistakes in sports.

Many Sports

In the seminary, and even out on the firing line, it is manifest that you can't learn the fine points of proper observance in the numerous sports available to the public — and this is not expected now or later. All the accepted code demands is that you know the behavior pattern of your favorite sport in the seminary and afterward when you play it as a priest.

Then again, not all seminarians are of the outdoor athletic type. There are those who prefer the indoor games, bridge, chess, checkers, bowling, billiards, etc. But here again each contest has its own peculiar behavior code which you are presumed to know before you enter into competition within or outside the seminary.

Incidentally, bridge has its own special rules of behavior which differ from those of other card games and competitive sports. Bridge is an exception to the general rule.

Learn the Code

Obviously the details of these various behavior codes cannot be covered in this treatise. You will have to look elsewhere for them. One excellent source which covers many of them in compact form is *New Esquire Etiquette for Men*. This book has a section on Sports — from billiards to golf; from horseback riding to yachting, and the proper etiquette for them and for club membership.

Golfing at a private club, member or guest, for instance, involves quite a different pattern of behavior than on a fee or public course. The emphasis here is that you must be thoroughly conversant with the particular sport code before you deal a hand or bait a hook. If you are in doubt, check with your sponsor before you serve a ball or tee up. It may save your reputation as a sportsman and you may be invited back. Now for your seminary sports.

In the Seminary

Your seminary outdoor games are strictly intramural, such as baseball, basketball, volleyball, hockey, touch football, etc. The type of game and style of play may differ in various geographical locations because of circumstances, popularity, and other causes. But the behavior pattern is constant.

Moreover the seminarian's outdoor games have an additional motivation over and above the "win" motivation of competitive sports. You, the seminarian, have the physical fitness element in mind — at least your superiors have — "a sane mind in a sound body" — as befits your future activity. You, aside from the physical development, have another important objective, through your group activity. It is to "relate" yourself with your classmates; to learn the practice of "give and take" in games; to observe the code of gentlemanly conduct in sports; to be a good loser and a graceful winner.

Your real character, your manliness, your justice, your square dealing, will all disclose themselves in play. There is no better place for exhibiting your seminary training than the athletic field. Here you will learn and practice the unwritten law of proper sports deportment. This knowledge and practice will prepare you for proper participation in public sports, be it pitching horseshoes, swinging golf clubs, or shooting rabbits. Your companions will joyfully label you "a right guy."

During the Summer

During your own training period in the minor or major seminary your summers and vacation periods will be spent at home, in summer school, or at work, but you probably will engage in team sports with local groups. In your earlier days it will be your regional popular team sport, baseball, hockey, basketball, etc. When you are more mature it may be golf, tennis, or some other individual sport.

In any event you will bring to your recreation the principles of fair play and good sportsmanship which you have learned and practiced in your seminary games. You will not stoop to any questionable practices which may be in vogue in that community, or which may be used by your local groups. At all times you will be a true sportsman and a considerate gentleman. Your conduct will be under observation and you will by your example reflect credit upon the institution you represent — your seminary.

Principles and Practice

Don't let all that has been said already in this chapter discourage your athletic ambitions. Observing the behavior code of your favorite sport will not make you a champion, but the practice of its ethics will be invaluable to you when you receive your first parish assignment. The venerable pastor has probably been waiting eagerly for your arrival, so that he can at once divest himself of the school's athletic program and hand it to you, the sturdy young assistant, so enthusiastic about sports (according to the bishop's report). And if you make good he may even reward you with his old set of golf clubs and arrange guest privileges at his exclusive country club.

In all probability the boys have been even more anxious than the pastor to have an active leader and "coach." Now your behavior pattern of propriety on the athletic field and your ideals of sportsmanship and fair play will have a practical test in your inspiration of these eager beavers. Your own training on the athletic field at the seminary will begin to pay off. You will teach them the unwritten law of sportsmanship.

The Unwritten Law

You have probably been wondering, "Well, what are these unwritten laws? Name some of them!" You can't be blamed for your impatience. To enumerate them may sound like "sermonizing" but that is not the intent. Here goes: all these examples which follow apply particularly to golf. The unwritten rules, however, have *general* application.

1. Never cheat in a game, for first of all it is culpable and you will later on probably hate yourself for doing it. Resist the temptation to lift the ball out of the rut or to tee it up in the rough. Also count that "practice" stroke behind the tree when you dubbed the shot.

If you need another deducible conclusion it is: you won't get away with it. Your opponent probably will be too gentlemanly to challenge you, but he surely will not play with you again; or if he has to, because of group pressure, you will be "suspect" and there will be no fun in the game.

2. Don't be a hypocrite. This goes two ways: if you win, don't play it down; that's what you were trying to do all the time — win. So accept the triumph gracefully and modestly. Talk about the game itself rather than your victory. Sympathize with the loser on his bad luck at the critical turn of the game. Don't replay that long putt on the fifteenth green; how

you lined it up; how you gave it the proper curve angle — he saw it the first time.

On the other side, if you are the loser, don't alibi for yourself. You are supposed to have played your best (you can't even be suspected of letting down). Compliment the winner gracefully and really mean it. If you haven't played your best, then you haven't been honest with your opponent and his victory will be ashes. Leave out the postmortems.

3. Don't talk the game — play it. One of the worst pests in golf (or any game) is the chitchatter, the prittle-prattler, who keeps up a constant stream of small, irrelevant chatter until you almost drown in the ensuing flood of words. If conversation or a monologue is your purpose you had better stay home and practice it on the tape recorder. Your opponent may take his game seriously, he may diligently be trying to improve it; he may want to concentrate on his approach shots, for instance. Let him set the conversation pace. If you have taken him out to the golf course to wheedle a favor out of him, you'd better turn off the pointed conversation until you're on the nineteenth hole. You'll have a better chance and a more receptive listener.

4. More briefly, but not less important are these unwritten laws:

Apologies: Leave them at home, don't bring them to the golf course. If your handicap is the maximum the other players will know what to expect of you. Just do the best you can without flagellating yourself or verbally thumping your breast.

Temper: Keep it under control. If your game is off, or your breaks bad, remember losing your temper is much worse than losing a ball — or a friend.

Advice: To other players. Give it when asked, but don't be too free with it. Let your opponent play his own game, and make his own mistakes. You're not the pro, you know. Your friend is not taking a lesson, he is playing a game.

Clowning: Don't try to be a buffoon. Your opponents are not on the fairways to be entertained. If you are using your clowning to cover up your poor game, your behavior is discourteous. You are supposed to play your best. No playful or jocular conduct will be accepted as a substitute.

Bets: If (after you are out of the seminary where gambling is forbidden) you bet on your game, pay up immediately. If you do not want to play for stakes, say so in the beginning, but do not welsh on your gentlemanly contract once you have agreed to it. Don't quibble. You got yourself into it.

Respect: Treat the golf course and its equipment with the same careful consideration you give to your own clubs. Replace divots, respect the greens.

The above is an attempt to put in print what every seminarian should know instinctively from his general training. The list is suggestive rather than comprehensive. If you find yourself in a situation where you are doubtful as to the correct procedure, then do the gentlemanly thing, the considerate thing, and you won't go wrong very far. But don't lose your temper; don't play rough; don't break your clubs . . . it wasn't the club's fault.

Your First Assignment — The Boys

After you have mastered the unwritten laws — and yourself, after they become a part of your "second nature," you will have more confidence when you approach your assistant's assignment in the parish with the big school. You will be more effective in passing on your experience and the unwritten principles of sportsmanship to the eager boys. You will know from having lived it yourself how to teach them true sportsmanship.

They will learn many things from you. Among them will be that the true sportsman is a good loser and a gracious winner; that games are won by teamwork; to play hard but fair; to play "heads-up"; to take advantage of the other team's mistakes or fumbles; to outsmart them, but not to resort to sharp practices; to be loyal to their team and their school.

These boys will learn from you not to try to get away with everything they can because they think the referee doesn't see. You will teach them that such boys display poor sportsmanship and they penalize their team when they do get caught; that courteous boys observe all the written rules of the game as well as the unwritten law of charity; that consideration of others is the final test; that "athlete's Head" is much more serious than "athlete's Foot"; not to be an "alibier" or a "boaster."

The Final Test

Finally, the way they play, as you know, will be a greater proof of their character training than their conduct in any other school activity. Teach them to keep their heads; to be gentlemen under all circumstances. You, the new assistant, will teach your grade school boys these and many other unwritten rules. And you will love doing it; it is a part of your apostolate.

You probably won't advert to it directly (certainly the boys won't) but sports can and should be a means for them to acquire many natural virtues, such as fortitude and courage, patience and perseverance. And you the coach, seminarian, or priest, must fulfill your apostolate in this respect by exhibiting these qualities yourself before you can impart them to the youngsters. With impressionable boys "example speaks louder than words."

The Reward

Then when they are ready for high school (or the junior seminary) they will have learned self-control, gentlemanliness, and consideration of others. Your patient and slow sowing of the seeds of proper sportsmanship will sprout and ripen in their future athletic endeavors. They will reap the harvest of your planting of the unwritten code — both athletically and scholastically; as present gentlemen and future adult citizens.

Chapter 11. WHEN SICKNESS COMES

At Home

If and when you, the junior seminarian who lives at home, become sick or incapacitated, so you are unable to attend classes and must remain home, house confined, it normally becomes the duty of your parents, or guardians, to assume the responsibility for your care during your sickness and for your convalescence during your recovery period.

They will be guided in your treatment by their experience in these matters and by the instructions of the physician if it is necessary to request his services.

The parents will advise the proper seminary authorities as to your illness, its character, and its probable duration. The authorities, in turn, will make whatever arrangements they deem proper for your home study during this period.

If you should become ill at the school, or meet with an accident there, and are sent home, you should be perfectly frank and candid with your parents in reporting the full details. It is false reasoning for you to attempt to disguise the facts in order to save your parents from worrying. The plain unvarnished truth in the matter of illness or accident is the only sensible course to follow with them. Then it will be possible for your parents to arrange for the proper treatment or professional consultation. Then your parents can keep the seminary authorities informed, for they are vitally interested in your condition.

You will be in good hands when you are ill at home. We

are concerned here with sickness when it comes to you away from home — at the seminary when you reside there. This phase of your possible illness or accident has several aspects which must be considered.

At the Seminary

When you catch a cold, develop a fever, have any illness, meet with an accident, if you are like most healthy young seminarians, your thinking becomes a bit warped at this new experience.

You will become introspective and inclined to consider only yourself and your comfort to the exclusion of the infirmarian and the community, the doctor and the hospital. Let us consider each of these categories in order.

Your Attitude

Your first reaction when sickness comes will probably be either that of a martyr bravely carrying your cross of inactivity, or that of the prisoner (confined to room or hospital — in "isolation") through no fault of your own, separated from your companions, your community and all its exercises. You'll feel sorry for yourself.

Resist the temptation to resort dramatically to heroics and bravado. Remember "heroics" may be dangerous if the illness covered up is serious. "I'll *not* go to bed or to the hospital. It's a waste of time. I don't want to miss classes. I've thrown off colds before. I'm strong! I can take it!"

But you've missed the point. Maybe *you* can take it, but can the *community* take it? Consideration of others is the first rule of etiquette, and charity is the bond that unites us in the seminary. Remember that you live in a community, and its welfare and its health are the first considerations. The members of the community, generally speaking, will observe the "bonds of charity" and will be understanding and considerate of your illness. But you must exercise the same charity.

The correct attitude for you when sickness comes was pronounced by an ancient Roman, quoted once before, Publius. It has become a popular maxim with the moral theologians through the ages. "No one should be the judge in his own cause (or case)." The seminary authorities and the physician are the ones to pass judgment on your illness, its diagnosis, and its treatment.

Hence, according to this rule, the question of staying up or going to bed, of isolation or hospital, for your ailment is not *your decision,* it is rather *your obedience.*

Just because you are miserable physically and disgruntled at your confinement to quarters or to the hospital is no reason why you should vent your displeasure on the infirmarian, the community, or the doctor. Earn some merit from the unpleasant situation by offering it up.

Try to be cooperative with the infirmarian, the doctor, and with visitors if they are permitted. Share your pleasure with them, but not your afflictions.

The Infirmarian

Infirmarians are selected by the seminary authorities with consideration for their ability to discharge the responsible duties of this assignment. The infirmarian is not a licensed physician (nor does he pose as such) but he is definitely an experienced colleague and he should be respected as one with authority to care for the sick.

The infirmarian is thoroughly conscious of his diagnostic limitations, but he is also perfectly aware of his ability to determine whether your indisposition will respond to local treatment or whether you should consult a physician. He is a competent "liaison officer," an intermediary, who should be respected for his official standing and for his sane judgment.

So you should consult the infirmarian when you require medication or bandaging. Do not diagnose your own case, nor prescribe for it. Do not try to cure yourself. Do not "shop around" among your classmates for proposed remedies. Go to the infirmarian who is experienced. He may save you much unnecessary suffering from "quack" medication or improper external applications. He will be able to determine whether you need the services of a physician or a surgeon.

When sickness comes to you inform the infirmarian promptly of your indisposition. If you are unable to get out of bed, have one of your companions notify the infirmarian, so he may take proper action: inform the superior, notify the house physician, or call an ambulance if it is an emergency, such as threatened appendicitis, or some crisis where time is of the essence.

If, however, you are on your feet, but indisposed, you must seek out the infirmarian, inform the superior, or consult a physician. You should not try to evade it by attempting to delegate it to the infirmarian. His duties do not extend to such personal responsibilities. These obligations belong to you personally and they are not transferable to the infirmarian.

In this connection your attention might also be called to the fact that the infirmarian is not an "appointment" secretary. Don't ask him to make your doctor or dental appointments for you. These personal engagements should receive your private attention. Incidentally, have your regular dental care during vacation. Again, this is your personal responsibility.

Medical Supplies

The infirmarian has charge of two types of medication: general and specific. They are usually kept in a medicine cabinet or closet available to the seminarian.

General items, such as anacin, aspirin, bufferin, sodium bicarbonate, gauze dressings, band-aids, adhesive tape, absorbent cotton, etc., are for common use and may be utilized freely by you, but see "Warning" below. However when you empty a bottle, or use the last of a dressing, you should make proper provision for calling attention to that fact, so that replacements may be supplied promptly.

Specific items in the medicine closet generally include such standard preparations as dermassage, liniments, ointments, laxatives, boric acid, syringes, heat pads, etc. These are for common usage but not for personal appropriation. If you take any of these items to your room you should return it promptly to the cabinet, or the infirmarian should be notified where it is in use. It just might happen that the infirmarian might have urgent need of that particular article which you have appropriated to yourself.

Warning: Your use of such items as aspirin, anacin, cathartics and similar "home remedies" should be occasional and moderate. The tendency among some seminarians, as observed by physicians, is to use these drugs excessively and over an extended period.

If you find that you are making regular and frequent trips to the general medicine closet then you need professional advice. You should acquaint the infirmarian with your specific condition and he in turn will determine whether the physician should be consulted.

Special Situations

The specific regulations for visiting the sick vary in different seminaries. In some seminaries there are infirmaries or isolation wards; in others there are sick sections; in some confinement is to the seminarian's own room.

Whatever is the special arrangement in your seminary for

the sick you will have your own visiting regulations. These rules should be observed rigorously. This is particularly true in isolation cases or epidemic times.

What is said here is intended to be suggestive to the "well" seminarian in the way of being helpful to the infirmarian and comforting to the patient, but it must be interpreted in consonance with the particular regulations of your own seminary.

In times of epidemic, flu, or a number of seminarians sick in bed at one time, you should give some thought to the overworked infirmarian. The following suggestions will aid him, help the sick, and increase your own self-respect if you put them into action — all in accordance with your particular regulations:

a) When several of your classmates are room confined, offer to carry one or more of the meal trays.

b) If a colleague has been sick for some time, offer to change his sheets and linens and to air his room while he sits in a chair. Both he and the infirmarian will appreciate your thoughtfulness.

c) Offer to take over the duty assignment of the sick seminarian.

d) In your charity visit the sick brethren. Make all visits brief especially if he has the flu, cold, or contagious disease. The visit may be a bit longer if it is a sprain, post operation, or broken bone case. But do all in accordance with your local regulations and do not prolong the visit.

e) Do not visit in large groups. The resulting noises and excitement may be bad for the patient and the fresh supply of air needed by the patient may be exhausted.

The Community

It is a common misconception for you, a seminarian, to think you are doing the community a favor by remaining in its midst with a bad cold, or other infectious or contagious disease. This fallacious reasoning works two hardships: to you and to the community.

Your failure to take proper early precautions for your malady can easily result in a secondary infection, a serious sickness, and a prolonged recovery. It is a shortsighted policy to neglect early symptoms — nature's warnings.

Your failure to give proper consideration to the community by secluding yourself when you have a contagious cough or a sneezing cold may have serious effects on others from contact with you.

In addition to the hazard of infecting others, you render the members of the community uneasy by your noticeable misery and by their apprehension of catching your germs.

The safe and the sane thing to do is to report to the infirmarian or the superior and then follow the advice given.

The Physician

It is well for you to remember that when the physician is called in you are requesting the services of an expert. He should be treated as an expert and his opinions and instructions should be followed accordingly.

You, as a seminarian, will receive the very best medical and surgical skills obtainable. Often some of these experts in their professional field have made their services available to the seminary on a gratuitous basis as a part of their contribution to the service of humanity. These professional men recognize the kindred service the Catholic priests are rendering and this is a reciprocal relationship.

If the doctor orders bed, hospital, or isolation, he is doing what in his expert opinion is best for your speedy recovery and for the community's welfare.

Be faithful in taking the medicine prescribed at the appointed times. The pills in the box or the medicine in the bottle will not improve your health unless taken internally — no matter how disagreeable the results may be. Follow the doctor's instructions carefully. Do not prolong medication or convalescence beyond the specified time.

Warning: Today there are many potent medications available to the medical profession. For your particular need your physician may prescribe one of these "miracle" drugs. However, frequently these drugs produce oblique effects. If the remedy prescribed for you produces disturbing side effects, or if a favorable response does not occur in the expected time, your physician should be informed of the facts.

This information is important to your physician and he will appreciate your disclosure. It will enable him to prescribe a different medication and to follow up your progress report more accurately.

Get up at once when the doctor orders you to do so. In neither case — going to bed or getting up — are you a competent judge in your own case.

Take the exercise prescribed, keep the diet ordered, rebuild your strength properly. Return to regular schedule, meals, classes, etc., as soon as possible. In other words, do not pamper yourself, but cooperate fully with your doctor.

The Hospital

When you are admitted to a hospital, remember you are a patient requiring medication and treatment, not a guest at a luxury hotel.

Today hospitals are overcrowded and the accomodations may be limited. Accept cheerfully what is available, whether ward, semiprivate, or temporary quarters.

If you are fortunate enough to secure a private room, show

your appreciation by obeying the regulations. Do not make a nuisance of yourself by demanding extra and superfluous attention.

If there is a telephone in your room (and there usually is) use it sparingly and mostly for emergency purposes. Do not use it for lengthy visits to your friends or relatives (you tie up one of the hospital's switchboard lines), nor for endless demands upon the telephone operator or the staff.

Treat your nurses with uniform courtesy. Remember these nurses are on duty to care for your essential needs and to render professional service. They are not there to take your capricious orders. You are only one of their numerous patients. Be considerate.

Do not ask the nurses embarrassing questions about your condition, operation, temperature, or length of stay. Professionally the nurses may not answer such questions. If you desire this information ask your doctor, not your nurse.

Above all you should not expect "star" treatment or "red carpet" consideration simply because you are a seminarian.

Do not be insistent in your demands and do not complain about the food or service. Remember the hospital staff wants you out of the hospital just as badly as you wish to go . . . maybe more so . . . for somebody is waiting for your bed . . . you are not a prisoner!

Whether patient or visitor keep this one thought in mind: the reputation of your diocese and superiors is in your hands when you are in a hospital.

If you forget everything else that has been set down here, try to shape your hospital code of conduct around these three words: acceptance; edification; gratitude.

Acceptance of your illness in a religious spirit.

Edification to staff and other patients by your virtue, your peace and resignation.

Gratitude for all that has been done for you by the doctors, interns, nurses, technologists, and attendants.

Visiting the Patient

Your conduct in the hospital as a visitor should be such that it fits into the orderly pattern of this highly organized institution.

You, the visitor, should always be courteous to Sisters, nurses, and other hospital personnel.

Make your visit brief and cheerful. Leave the patient rested and encouraged. Don't worry him about your seminary or class affairs, or current gossip. The burden of good behavior is your responsibility, not the patient's.

If the patient is in a ward or a semiprivate room you should remember that the other patients are ill and do not disturb them by your loud talking or your smoking.

You can control your impulse to smoke until after your brief visit, even if the patient is in a private room.

All hospitals have definite visiting rules. The hours are specified and the number of visitors at any one time is strictly limited. Do not presume upon your clerical state or your Roman collar to flaunt these rules.

Do not sit on the patient's bed (or for that matter sit on any bed). Do not place overcoat, topcoat, hat, gloves, etc., on the bed. Hold them if necessary. If there are not sufficient chairs remain standing for your visit will be short.

Do not be boisterous in your visit. Do not disturb the routine of the hospital or of the patient. Observe the regulations. They are made for the efficient operation of the hospital and the benefit of the patients.

Your Roman collar will be respected by the staff and attendants. They will be reluctant to enforce rigid visiting rules upon you. Do not make it necessary for them to do so.

Observe the standard rules of visiting hours, number of visitors at one time, silence or quietness, and any other local regulations.

Observe a dignified but cheerful demeanor in your relations with the staff, Sisters, doctors, nurses, attendants, but do not assume a frigid aloofness which prohibits a passing nod, or a pleasant "good morning," or a cordial smile from any of the staff. Your icy manner will be resented by the hospital officials and the priesthood will suffer from the unfavorable impression thus created.

Be natural, be yourself, be cheerful. The staff see enough misery and suffering. Lift the load a little bit by your pleasant manner.

Here is a reminder if you have a priest visitor when you are confined to the hospital. Ask him for his blessing before he leaves. If you have other visitors when he calls be sure to introduce them to him.

Chapter 12. WHEN THE LADIES ARE PRESENT

Present Limitations

I. At Home

Your social relations with young women while you are living at home will be severely limited. You are not the normal high school pupil or college student with his social freedom of proms and dating. You are a seminarian preparing for the priesthood. You will restrict your social recreation in accordance with your ideals and in conformity with your institution's regulations.

II. During Vacations

During your major seminary years your social relations with women will be even more decidedly limited. Your summers will be more or less occupied with seminary vacational activities, camp, club, Catholic Action, social work, guidance, group moderator, etc.

You have your specific regulations from the seminary guiding your summer activities and your conduct. These are established and traditional. You will, naturally, observe them rigorously, so they need no elaboration or comment here in this book.

III. At the Seminary

While you are at the major seminary during the school year you will meet with your relatives, the relatives of your classmates, the Sisters of the institution, and occasional visitors. Most of these meetings will take place in the seminary parlor or on the seminary grounds. At other times you will be in the company of women in public conveyances, stores, and possibly at sports events.

These following rules are intended to cover the general situations you will encounter during your years of study in which the "fair sex" may be involved. For a complete formula of social regulations after your ordination you are respectfully referred to the complete *New Esquire Etiquette*, which should be available in your students' libraries.

The classification and the headings which follow are those of *Esquire*. They have been used so that you may not be confused when you refer to the complete manual.

There is some repetition of what has been said elsewhere in this book, but this is intentional so that you may have ready reference in this one place.

Your Head

Take your hat off whenever you are indoors, whether women are in sight or not. This "indoors" includes not only homes but apartment-house elevators and corridors; also all eating places. Reserved space on trains, dining cars, and airplanes is also considered "indoors."

Public buildings, department stores and their elevators are *not* considered "indoors." Neither are local or suburban trains, hotel lobbies, railroad and airplane waiting rooms "hats off" places.

But if other male occupants of public elevators or places remove their hats, you should conform even though you may be socially correct in keeping your hat on. It isn't sufficiently important to make an issue of it, or to draw attention to yourself.

Take your hat off *outdoors* when you stop to talk to a woman. But if you remain talking or join her in walking replace your hat. Convention formerly required that your head remain uncovered, but common sense prevails today. The hat-in-hand routine appears too much as though you are soliciting a contribution for your favorite charity. She will appreciate it if you put your hat on after observing the formalities.

Take it off when you have your photograph taken with your relatives or visitors.

Lift it momentarily to the lady when you acknowledge her greeting or good-bye. Lift it when you perform some service even for a strange woman, such as picking up something she has dropped, and for all brief exchanges with women, known or unknown.

If a man, accompanied by a woman, salutes you in passing, lift your hat in return. Even if the man is alone and he raises his hat to you in respect to your clerical state, return the courtesy. Even if a little boy greets you with a smile and a courteous touch of his cap (or a little girl nods at you) the very least you can do, seminarian or priest, is to return the smile and greeting and raise your hat. There is no age limit, up or down, for your display of proper manners. You will never know what effect your gracious manners may have on that little boy's (or girl's) future! In any event you have been the courteous gentleman.

Your Eyes

It should hardly be necessary to tell a seminarian that no gentleman rudely stares at a woman; nor does he inventory her with appraising eyes. This comment is included here so that the record may be complete.

Women have a "sixth sense" — they intuitively know when

they are in "candid-camera" focus. When you are, therefore, on the street or wherever women are present, you will "keep your eyes to yourself." A seminarian knows from his training and his own refined discrimination what is proper and fitting in the custody of the eyes, for the eye is the mirror of the soul. The point need not be labored.

Your Feet

When you are seated and a woman enters your seminary parlor, or the living room of your family home, you rise to your feet instantly and remain standing until she is seated. But don't make it ostentatious and don't make a jumping jack of yourself if women are passing in and out of the room.

If you are seated at a theater (or in chapel), stand up when others are trying to pass in front of you to reach their seats in the same row. You only complicate matters if you remain seated and try to jackknife your knees. They can't squeeze past you, and you will ultimately have to rise, so do it in the beginning.

The same principle applies to a crowded elevator. If you are in the front and someone in the back is trying to get off, step out of the elevator to make room. Or if both you and a woman are getting off on the same floor and you are in front, the sensible thing for you to do is to get off first. The same practice is followed in taxicabs and automobiles. Do the easiest and quickest thing — the sensible thing.

Walk on the street side of the sidewalk if you are accompanying a woman. This is standard practice. But don't be a stickler for form if you have to shift positions frequently. The rule is: keep the woman or women (if there are two of them) on the inside or on your right, but only if you can avoid awkward shuffling. It isn't so important that you must make a "cause célèbre" out of it.

The rule that women precede men through doors is a set one, except that a man goes ahead if the couple is walking the length of a train, opening the heavy doors and holding them open until the woman passes through. He also goes ahead in a restaurant if the head waiter is not there to seat them.

A woman, however, passes through a revolving door first after the man has set it in motion for her.

On a fixed stairs, the man precedes the lady up the stairs, but follows her down.

On an escalator the process is reversed for safety reasons. The man follows the lady on a stairs moving up; precedes her coming down.

Your Hands

Don't offer your hand to a woman when you are introduced, unless she extends hers first. If she does offer her hand, don't pump it, or crush it, or bear-trap it. Remember she probably has rings on her fingers.

If you are introduced on the street and the lady extends her hand, remove your glove before shaking hands with her *only* if you can do it inconspicuously and without delay. (See chapter on Introductions.) It is obviously inconsiderate of you to leave her hand dangling in midair while you remove a glove, finger by finger. This situation simulates the "indoor" circumstances where you do not have on a glove. The lady expects you to be gloved on the street when she extends her hand. So do the obvious thing: take her gloved hand in yours without creating a scene. Don't say "excuse my glove." It sounds "prissy" and it is almost a slap at the lady's graciousness in offering her hand.

You give your hand, palm up, to a woman to help her

off buses and out of cabs. In these situations, you precede her so that you can be in a position to help.

The conventional form of offering your arm in any circumstances, except the above bus or cab situation, has about gone out of practice. Women, as a rule, do not like to be touched needlessly.

Only in some emergency, such as a loss of balance, a break or hole in the sidewalk, an approaching car unsighted by her, do you venture to support her or guide her. She will appreciate your assistance at such times. But let her step off curbs and cross streets under her own power.

Three Rules

There are three general rules which you can follow in most normal situations, but they all admit of common sense interpretation and obvious exceptions. They are:

1. Ladies First

This is the general rule. It applies, for instance, when there is a waiter to lead you to a table, an usher to lead you to your seats, or a doorman to open the taxi door. But when there is no waiter nor usher you go first to find the table or the seats. When the doorman is busy or inattentive you take over and hold the door for the lady. When the way is clear and free naturally, the lady goes first, but if you have to mill through a crowd, or elbow your way through a rush, or a high step is to be vaulted, then you "run interference."

In a word, you go first when there is a good reason for reversing the regular order.

2. Hold All Doors

Here again this is a general rule, but at times it presents

some difficulties, requires some dexterity, and at other times it defies all regulations. Moreover you cannot, in this age of modernity, be sure how the athletic young Miss may respond to your chivalrous action.

With the "ladies first" she will arrive at the door slightly ahead of you and she may grasp the doorknob herself with physical might, so the best you can do is to finish the job.

But whatever happens on the first door, be prepared for surprises. She may stand demurely and helplessly at the second door waiting for your manly strength to perform the operation so she can pass through gracefully.

Your task is to be ready and alert for any emergency and to try to anticipate her specific reaction at each new contingency.

You have to develop a nice sense of timing and casualness — if you are going to be helpful rather than hampering. But don't expect to work out any general rules from your past experiences. It just won't work out into a definite pattern. You will have to be flexible enough and resourceful enough to meet new predicaments with complete composure — and timely alertness.

3. Hold All Chairs

Here again it is the gesture that counts, whether she sits down or arises. She probably will slide into the chair before you can render any practical assistance, but don't commit the blunder of omitting the gesture. She will take it amiss.

Your best procedure will be always to walk around behind her chair, to help her off with her coat, and to make one final adjustment of her chair. Just see that she is seated before you go back to your place.

In reverse order, the technique is the same when she rises — just get the chair out of her way when she steps out

of it and don't push it back under the table until she is completely free of it. You will improve with practice. So we
finally come to an important warning.

Your Ears

Naturally, you will want to believe what every woman says,
but prudence will soon teach you that there are some circumstances when you must not believe your ears. For instance,
you will *want* to take her at her word when she says certain
things, but it is good manners *not* to do so. Here are some
examples:

"Please don't get up," or if you have struggled to your
feet *"Please sit down."* Don't follow her instructions, no
matter how much she protests. The rule you have seen in
the beginning of this chapter requires that you stand while she
stands. No protest on her part can change that and if you do
not live up to your good manners, she is going to be offended.

Another one: *"Don't bother, I can manage."* She probably
can, whether it is opening a bottle of soda, or moving a
chair. But if you stand by nonchalantly and let her struggle,
she will think poorly of your manners and you are going to
look pretty silly to the people who didn't hear her *"Don't
bother."*

A final example: *"You go ahead; I'll be all right."* Don't
do it, whatever it involves. She doesn't really want to be left
alone. It will be simpler all around for you to see it through.
It is your duty and it will save future complications.

Summary

So to recapitulate: when it comes to the world of women,
etiquette is everything. This was demonstrated in a survey in
cities from coast to coast by *This Week,* a national newspaper

magazine. It disclosed that the women were bothered most by "men's table manners."

Number one on the list of protests was men's failure to seat women guests first at table in a restaurant, something covered in this chapter (3. Hold All Chairs). High in the complaints about "men's mistakes" were: men ordered their own food first; men complained about the service; men slurped soup and coffee; men sprawled; chewed with mouth open; talked while chewing; did not pass food . . . mostly table manners, but also mentioned prominently was "do not hold doors open."

To conclude: You just can't break social rules by your rugged individualism or by your coarse idiosyncrasies. You will not be excused on account of your years of isolation from social activity.

On the contrary, your clerical state and your formal education will be considered as supreme preparation for your social life and its proprieties. You will be expected to be models of the social virtues. You must not fail the public in its concept of your training and your aptitude.

It is a part of your apostolate.

Chapter 13. THE AUTOMOBILE

General

Each seminary, minor and major, has its own regulations regarding the use, operation, or ownership of automobiles during school terms and vacation periods.

These rules also govern, according to local circumstances, the use (or prohibition) of cars for transportation to and from school when the seminarian lives at home.

These local regulations also specify the conditions for the use of seminary automobiles, trucks, and tractors by the seminarians both inside and outside the seminary grounds.

The only comment here is: know your regulations and obey them.

Protection

Generally all seminary authorities caution their students, either expressly or inferentially, against the use of uninsured automobiles. In a few states (Wisconsin, Massachusetts, Colorado) insurance is compulsory, but in the vast majority it is not.

If when you are home you drive the family car (or any other automobile) you should have your official driver's license and the car should be covered by proper insurance (property damage and personal liability). The insurance should also provide proper protection for you, a nonowner, when you drive the car which you do not own.

It is a fact that driving habits are the basis for high

automobile insurance costs. For instance, one class of applicants who finds it difficult to secure auto insurance is the single male under 25. Unfortunately you, the seminarian, fall into this class, irrespective of your driving ability and law observance.

Under 25 Years

Some insurance companies will not insure the single male under 25. Other companies do not like to insure him, and all who do will give him protection only at a much higher rate than for other classifications.

These restrictions, or limitations, arise from the fact that this age group has the highest percentage of fatal accidents and bodily injuries; also the greatest number of car and property damages.

A major reason for these high insurance rates for this age group (under 25) is that these youngsters are considered the reckless drivers, the "drag" racers, the "souped-up" car owners, the "hot-rod" drivers and the dare demons.

Neither you (nor any sane seminarian) is going to risk life, limb, or vocation against being called "chicken" for refusing to participate — even as a "guest" — in such cars and contests. The seminarian doesn't need any rules spelled out for such refusal.

Another Cause

Other causes for high insurance rates for all classifications are the dishonesty on the part of otherwise honest people who make exaggerated (or false) claims for bodily injuries, and the connivance to bilk the insurance companies on claims.

The caution here is for you, the seminarian, to make certain you know the state and local laws regarding responsibility wherever you drive; that you conduct yourself properly if you are involved in an accident (see below); and that you are fully covered by insurance before you get behind the steering wheel.

In case of seminarians driving rented cars for group trips to or from the seminary on vacation periods, holiday trips, etc., it is assumed that the rental agency, if reliable, carries the proper protection for the car and you, the driver. But this should be verified in each case.

Your Own Accidents

If you cause an accident to a parked car, for instance, if you dent its fender while you are squeezing in a space, do the proper thing: find the owner, or leave your name and address in the damaged car. Then report the accident to your insurance company through the proper channels.

In more serious accidents, to a moving vehicle or to a person, whether you are at fault or not, be courteous. Do not become involved in any heated arguments. Secure the driver's name, the car license, etc.; give the same information about your car and insurance; obtain the names of any witnesses and avoid controversy. Report the accident to the police and/or the Motor Vehicle Department. *But do not leave the scene of the accident.*

If personal injuries are involved to anyone in the accident render what assistance you can physically (and spiritually), then await the arrival of the police officials. Again, do not leave the scene of the accident and do not lose your poise as a seminarian.

Important Caution

From what has been said (above) about dishonest people in case of accidents, or through subsequent conspiracy or collusion with "ambulance chasers," garage owners, shyster lawyers, and eventually unpredictable juries, it becomes imperative for you, the seminarian, involved in any kind of an accident, no matter how trivial it may seem at the time, to remain on the scene of the accident. You should get a police report before the cars are moved and you should endeavor to obtain names and addresses of witnesses. These precautions are necessary in order to protect yourself against subsequent and exorbitant claims for personal injuries. It can happen. It has happened. It may happen to you!

Avoiding Accidents

Accidents don't *happen*. They are *caused*. They are caused by human errors, by mechanical failures, or by weather conditions.

Overcautiousness is the cause of many accidents. Slow driving in highway traffic, especially on expressways where the *minimum* speed is posted, is as dangerous as excessive speed in zoned districts. Keep within the regulated high and low limits and keep up with the traffic.

Here are a few suggestions for avoiding accidents:

A. Driving is a full time job, so don't let your conversation with your front seat companion get too involved or intent. Keep your mind (and your eyes) on the road. Your traveling companion will understand your concentration — he drives too.

B. If you are driving a long distance, especially if you are alone, beware of "fatigue driving." If you catch yourself with head nodding or eyes closing, the remedy is to break up the monotony with a "coffee break," a pause off the road for a leg stretch, or some diversion at least every 100 miles, or less if you notice the symptoms. Variety or change, even a few minutes, will be a safety factor. Use seat belts.

C. Here are three road prohibitions mentioned in all "rules of the road":

1. If you drink, don't drive; if you drive, don't drink.
2. Alcohol and gasoline don't mix.
3. Don't take that last drink "for the road."

These injunctions are mentioned here not by way of implication, but so that this list of "Suggestions" may be complete.

Rules of Driving

This is not the place for a statement of the "Rules of the Road." You were supposed to know them when you applied for your license and took your driver's test. If you need a refresher course you can obtain these regulations from your state agency, automobile associations, insurance company, or at the corner gas station.

The emphasis here is on the intangibles. For instance, the qualities which will make you a fine driver are essentially the same personality factors which make you a gentleman. If you display the same mannerly courtesy on the road that you manifest in other social relations you will never deliberately violate the rules of the road.

Driving Manners

You don't need this etiquette book to tell you that a *safe* driver is a *good* driver; that a sensible driver doesn't take chances.

You don't need a theologian to tell you "Obey traffic laws"; "Don't be angry"; "Don't be rude"; "Don't make others lose their tempers."

Besides a tank of gas when you turn on that ignition key, what you really need is the good lubricant of introspection.

Here are a few "tune-up tests" which you can self-administer. They will help you to determine your driving "I.Q." and your "Achievement" rating.

Self-Inventory

1. If behind the wheel you apply the Golden Rule of conduct mentioned by St. Luke: "Even as you wish men to do to you, so also do you to them" the chances are you will not raise your blood pressure or irritate your ulcers; nor cause similar alarming symptoms in other drivers. And you will greatly reduce the hazard of accidents.

2. On the road today (and tonight) simple self-preservation demands that you have your best party manners with you when you put your car into gear — in other words consideration of others.

3. Drive carefully where children are at play. Stop to allow pedestrians to cross. Stop to allow waiting cars to cross. Keep car clean, inside and outside.

4. "Self-preservation" means more than saving your own life or preventing accidents. Here is where the positive overtones of "introspection" enter. You can mentally (or vocally) "damn" the poor driving and bad manners of the other driver, but you won't reform him by your imprecations. So, for your own safety and peace of mind, don't let your annoyance show by pressure on the horn, or by leaning out the window to give him a curt lesson in driving. Philosophize instead. Be grateful that your presence of mind and your quick reactions prevented an accident.

5. Reason in this manner quite apart from the havoc, hatred, and danger which rudeness arouses on the road:

   a) I'm not going to let any ill-mannered motorist drive *me* crazy, so that I forget my good driving manners and jeopardize my safety and the car.

b) I am resolved to be meticulous in my observance of safety rules and traffic regulations; but at the same time I am going to be prepared for the worst violations of these laws from other drivers.

c) I know that the highways are crowded with stupid and reckless and show-off drivers who probably think they are the world's best. Of course, I'm not in that classification, but I'm going to be alert to the possible transgressions of others . . . and I'm not going to risk my safety or car because "I have the right of way." That won't be any consolation to me in the emergency room of the hospital, if I'm fortunate enough to be carried there instead of to the morgue.

Hitchhikers and Stops

Here are some important safety or "self-preservation" comments:

A. Picking up hitchhikers is forbidden by law in some states, and it is a dangerous practice in any state. There is no valid reason for you to stop your car at a signal from anyone you do not know except for a police officer.

When strangers, a serviceman in uniform or a citizen in apparent distress, are involved your own self-preservation supersedes all normal rules of etiquette. This simple rule is: "Do not stop for strangers."

B. Hold-up men will fake a car breakdown. Thugs will display distress signs. You can blink your lights, or sound your horn, to indicate that you have noted their plight, real or assumed. Then you can stop at the next gas station and report the incident. This is the kindest thing you can do — and it is the safest for you.

C. However, later on, as a priest, if there has been an accident where bodily injuries may be involved, you should stop to ascertain if you can render any spiritual assistance.

Your safe clue in this situation will be that other cars and people will already be on the scene.

D. In another emergency, if you are close enough to an accident to see it occur, or if you see a car leave the road then you have a different contingency in which your Good Samaritan offices are a recognized necessity.

Traffic Tickets

It is a curious fact that many otherwise law-abiding people feel that they can break traffic laws with impunity. You need only review your own experiences in this matter to determine your degree of guilt, if any. In any event, here are a few broad hints:

If you receive a traffic ticket for speeding, overparking, or any other infraction, treat the officer with courtesy. He is only doing his duty. Answer his questions quietly and hand him the papers he asks for — your license, car registration, etc.

Take your license card out of its holder in your purse before you present it. Do not be so thoughtless as to offer the officer your wallet with the card in it. This is tantamount to offering him a bribe. Do not place him in this embarrassing position but remove the card yourself from the wallet and present it alone to the officer retaining the purse in your own possession.

And a final admonition: you may be entirely right in the whole matter, but do not try to make the officer a judge in the matter. His jurisdiction does not extend to the court. Save your explanations (or defense) for the proper place.

Your Reward

As an encouragement to you to strive for an "A" in driving and a "zero" in accidents, for good marks in the observance of these simple rules and for freedom from traffic tickets, constantly remind yourself that the day is not far distant when you will be ordained.

Then you will have reached that maturity when you will graduate from the "under 25" penalty rate of insurance. Then you will become the proud owner of your own little domestic or foreign compact (after a few more payments).

With this ownership you will acquire a new sense of responsibility and you will be thankful that you learned and observed these few simple rules. Now it will pay off, for in the process of practicing them during your seminary days you will have become a safe driver, a good driver, a sensible driver. So now in your new classification as an "owner" you will be better qualified mentally and mechanically to take good care of your new car and its snappy appearance.

Chapter 14. TELEPHONE USAGE

In the Seminary

The use of the telephone for incoming and outgoing messages is strictly limited in all seminaries, major and minor.

Each institution has its own rules to fit its particular circumstances, but generally, the seminarian can receive only emergency incoming calls. Outgoing messages are limited to certain times and usually from a pay station or booth telephone.

The proper procedure for you to follow is to respect the regulations of your particular seminary; to obtain the required permission; to limit your calls as to number, times, and duration.

This limited use of the telephone itself, however, should not affect your knowledge and practice of the accepted code of telephone behavior. Indeed the very fact that your actual usage of the telephone will be so limited during your seminary days becomes an important reason for you to learn and to put into practice the fundamental requirements of proper telephone etiquette. You may have many more opportunities to practice these conventions during your vacation periods, at home, at work, at recreation, than you have at the seminary.

In many seminaries the students act as switchboard operators for the telephone equipment. If you are one of these, the following comments are of vital importance to you in fulfilling your duties properly and courteously.

You, however, should familiarize yourself with the rules

whether you are called on to operate a switchboard or not. The day will come all too soon when you will have to exercise these courtesies in a very definite manner in your priestly assignment.

General

The one simple and workable rule for telephone propriety is the "face-to-face" principle. Here it is: *Use the same courtesy toward the one who rings your telephone bell as you do toward the person who rings your doorbell.* This is fundamental. If this rule is observed all other details will fall into their proper place.

When you answer the doorbell and speak face to face with someone, your smile, your grooming, your warm personality combine to create a good impression.

When you answer the telephone this impression depends entirely upon your *voice,* so make your voice a pleasant one. The telephone companies stress the "voice with a smile" with their employees. You can develop a "voice with a smile" in your telephone answering and conversations.

The secret of getting that smile into your voice is *feeling* it. Ever notice how dead the mechanical voices taped into some services leave you? For example, when you dial a number and hear: "This is a recording — the number you have reached is not in service at this time. Please be sure you are calling the correct number." Ever notice how irritating that voice is even though the mistake was your own? Well, if *your* telephone voice is mechanical, it will never make a good impression on others.

If you stop to think how your voice may sound to someone on the other end of the wire, who may not even know you at all, you would certainly try to make your voice create a good impression.

You may not feel sunny and cheerful; you may even feel cold and grouchy; but whoever is at the other end of the wire can't know your feelings — he can only hear how your voice sounds. Your real personality, not your feelings, must come through to him! That becomes the warm smile in your cheerful voice. It is contagious! Cultivate it!

People who call the rectory telephone number expect a prompt and businesslike answer in a distinct and pleasant voice. Who knows, it may be the bishop calling! If you answer all incoming calls as you would the bishop's (if you knew he was calling), then you will create a good impression.

A Private Test

You might make a little private test to determine the quality of your answering voice:

1. Is it pleasant, friendly, cordial, cheerful, and interested? Then it has personality and the tone shows it. Such a voice is like a warm handshake over the telephone.

2. Is it expressionless, mechanical, indifferent, impatient, and listless? Then it lacks personality and creates the impression, "Oh, why bother me?" It's like slamming a door in the face of the caller. Remember it is not only *what* you say, but *how* you say it.

But don't be discouraged if you failed the above test. You can cultivate a good telephone voice by conscious and persistent practice. Then the final test will be when you notice that your pleasant voice brings a pleasant response from the one calling. Then you won't have to practice any longer — you've acquired it, and it will remain with you, and answering the telephone will be a pleasure for you and for the one calling. Now here are some specific rules to keep in mind.

Receiving Calls

I. Answer Promptly

When the seminary or rectory telephone rings, get the conversation off on the right track by answering promptly. You are going to have to answer it anyhow, so why delay? Besides it may be a sick call or some emergency.

II. Identify Your House

While "hello" is quite proper for a private home, the only correct identification greeting when you answer is: (for example) "St. John's Seminary." Or if you are receiving an incoming call on a switchboard say (for example) "Good morning, St. John's Seminary."

But this identification must be given in a slow, clear, distinct "at-your-service" voice so that it is understood at once by the caller. The common fault here is, if you are entrusted with answering the telephone as a regular duty, you will tend to slur the words together and mumble them indistinctly from much repetition so that the caller has to ask, "Is this St. John's Seminary?" Thus the conversation gets off to a limping start and it is difficult to get it into proper stride. So, always introduce yourself or your seminary, or your rectory in an intelligible manner.

III. Take Calls Courteously

If the priest asked for does not answer his telephone or his call signal, give the caller this information at once. Come back on the line and say: "I am trying to reach Father. Please hold on."

If you are unable to reach Father after a reasonable interval say, "I'm sorry I cannot reach Father just now." Then you can offer the caller a choice of two alternatives: "Do you wish to call back or shall I give Father a message?"

If the priest asked for is unable to answer the telephone call, give the caller a sufficient explanation, as: "I'm sorry, Father is in class"; or "Father is talking on another line"; or "Father is busy in the parlor just now."

Then give the caller a choice of waiting, or being called back, as "Do you wish to hold the line, or may I have Father call you?"

But if he chooses to wait, do not leave him dangling indefinitely. Come back on the line repeatedly and say: "I'm sorry, Father is still busy," or "It seems that Father is going to be detained some time. May I have him call you back?" In any event, don't permit the caller to get the impression that you have forgotten all about him.

If you know that Father is away, or if you are informed to that effect by the one who does answer your call, just say, "I'm sorry, but Father is not here now. Do you wish to talk to somebody else, or do you care to leave a message?" You are not supposed, as a switchboard operator, to know how long Father will be away or where he has gone. Do not volunteer that information, but say, "May I connect you with another Father?"

One real test of your courteous answering will be when, maybe, the telephone rings in the middle of the night. You jump out of bed thinking it is an emergency or a sick call. You hear some thick inebriated voice on the other end, "Is that you, Nellie?" Or maybe it is an honest mistake in dialing from a dark booth. Here is the test: Don't slam the receiver down in rage! Practice that virtue of self-control you've been making the point of your particular exam — then, with magnificent restraint say: "I'm afraid you have the wrong number.

This is St. Patrick's Rectory, COlumbia 9-7000," and place the receiver gently on the hook. You'll sleep better!

IV. Take Messages Accurately

Keep your pad and pencil available for taking messages. Many rectories have printed forms for this purpose.

Request, rather than *demand* information, as "May I tell Father who's calling?" "Do you care to leave your telephone number?"

Get the complete information and repeat it back to the caller to make sure it is correct: Name, number, city (if different from your own), date, and time.

Then one thing more: Don't trust your memory, or the fact that you will see Father at suppertime. See that the written message is put in his mailbox or on his door.

Whatever the circumstances, don't leave the caller waiting indefinitely without coming back on the line. Tell him promptly, "I'm sorry, I can't locate Father right away. Do you wish to leave your number, or will you call back?" This gives the caller an option in case he does not wish to give his name.

V. Handle Complaints Tactfully

You personally may in no way be involved in the complaint, but you represent the seminary or the rectory, so accept the complaint as a representative of the priesthood.

Be a good listener and remain calm and friendly. Avoid blaming somebody else or taking the matter as a personal affront.

Adopt a pleasant and helpful attitude. Apologize sincerely for mistakes, as "I am sorry that happened." Be ready to volunteer information and to offer assistance.

Leave the impression that you are truly concerned and

hopeful that such mistakes will not occur again. Let the complainer feel when he hangs up that his mission has been accomplished. He will feel better and so will you.

VI. Give Information Considerately

When callers seek information about church services, hours of confessions, or other matters, which you may have to look up, tell them so, as "Will you hold the line, please, while I look that up?" (Do not say, "Just a minute" or "Hold on.")

If you have to obtain the information from somebody else, say: "I am sorry but I do not have that information, but if you care to wait I'll try to find out for you."

If seeking the information is going to take you away from the line for considerable time, return to the line and report to the caller, as: "I'm still checking on that. Will you wait further, or may I call you back?"

Give the impression to the caller that you are glad to be of service. If you cannot obtain the desired information express your regret with sincerity.

NOTE: If you must set the receiver down to look up the information, be considerate of the person at the other end. Do not slam the hand phone down on the hard surface of the desk, but place it gently on a book or a pad. To set the receiver down slam-bang on the desk results in an unpleasant noise in the other person's ear and doesn't improve his disposition when you return with the information.

VII. Embarrassing Situations

There are times when it is practically impossible for you to answer the phone. For instance, you should not receive messages when they interrupt someone who has first call on your time. If you are busy in the parlor, giving an instruction, listening to a visitor with a problem, it is obviously impossible for you to conduct a conversation of some length on the telephone.

You cannot leave the people stranded in the parlor. They have first claim on your time, like the patients in a doctor's reception room — the first to arrive have priority.

If you have no switchboard operator to handle the call, but have to answer the telephone yourself, the very least you can do is to say to the person in the parlor, "I'm sorry" in genuine contrition before picking up the phone.

And then you should ask the telephoner if you may call him back at another time. "May I call you back?" means as clearly as if you said it outright: "I'm sorry, I can't talk now."

Let the caller know when you will call him back. And then you are honor bound to do it.

VIII.   Leaving Messages

If you leave a message (in case you cannot reach "Mr. Smith" personally) always leave your name, telephone number, city from which you are calling, and the reason for your call: "This is Father McCadden, I'm calling about the information he requested (or this is a personal call). I'm at SHeridan 9-6472, Johnston City, until noon (or specified time)."

Few things are more annoying to a busy man or to a priest than a message which says only "Call SH 8-8724." If you leave a message for Mr. Smith or Father Jones to return your call, cue him in as to what you are calling about. Don't let him call back into an unsuspected trap.

Better still, find out, if you can do so gracefully, when Mr. Smith will be in and do your own calling back. But if you have left your name and Mr. Smith doesn't call back, you may reasonably assume that Mr. Smith's failure to return your call has some reason, or he didn't get your message.

Then, if you *must* call again don't ask: "Didn't you get my message?" But rather, "I've been away from my room (or office), or my line has been busy, and I was afraid you may have been trying to reach me." This way you give Mr. Smith an out.

Placing Calls

1. Local Business Calls

Directory: If you are not sure of the telephone number, look it up in the directory. Do not trust your memory unless it is a number you call frequently.

You may keep numbers called frequently in a memo book. Your local telephone company will often provide a book, without charge. Again, don't trust your memory unless it is photogenic. Listen for the dial tone and then dial the letters and numbers carefully.

Wrong Numbers: If you make a mistake in dialing and you get an incorrect number, be gentlemanly about it, as: "I am sorry, *I* dialed the wrong number." Do not abruptly hang up without explanation. After all, you caused the inconvenience to the other person. Manfully acknowledge it.

Courtesy: When the called person answers, be as courteous as though he had opened his front door to your ring, the face to face courtly politeness.

If your call is answered by someone other than the person you are calling, give the name of the person you want to talk to, and your own name, if requested, "This is Father Matthew." Ordinarily you do not give her your name unless she is a "call-screener" as well as a switchboard operator. If she indicates she would like to have your name, give it promptly without quibbling: "This is Father Matthew."

Protocol: When the operator connects you to a telephone, you give your name at once, as: "This is Father Matthew. May I speak to Mr. Smith, please?"

You do this even if you suspect it is Mr. Smith who has answered. To start out with the blunt "Mr. Smith?" puts Smith on the defensive, for you have not introduced yourself and he may be avoiding some annoying calls.

Action: Then get on with your business at once. It is not a social call. Don't try to "warm up" Mr. Smith with a rash of persiflage about his health, his descendants, the weather — this may be normal procedure in oriental countries but not in practical, businesslike U. S. A. Get to the point. Mr. Smith, a busy man, will appreciate it.

Attitude: During the conversation, remember Mr. Smith can't see you. He can't read your lips, so speak clearly and distinctly.

If you are interrupted by anything short of a fire, even if the pastor drops in for some urgent information (he may have someone on his private line) explain the matter to Mr. Smith, as: "I'm sorry, Mr. Smith, I am interrupted. May I call you back?" Don't leave Mr. Smith in a vacuum while you give your attention to another matter. He won't be in a very good frame of mind when you come back to the telephone.

Blunders: If you have to "look something up" while you are talking to Mr. Smith, you have "pulled a boner." You should have had that information at hand before you placed the call. Again, do not keep Mr. Smith waiting on a dead line while you explore your files. Tell him: "I'm sorry, Mr. Smith, I'll have to check on that. May I call you back?"

Cut-Offs: Though being cut off in this day of almost universal dial service is extremely uncommon, it may occasionally happen. Don't fume, or try to place the blame — you will only agitate yourself. Wait a moment and then redial. The person you are calling will have hung up too and will be awaiting your reconnection.

Sign-Off: Since you initiated the call to Mr. Smith, it is your responsibility to end it. When you have completed your business with Mr. Smith, terminate the conversation with a courteous "Good-bye." Wait for his answering "Good-bye" before you replace the receiver. Don't slam the receiver back into its cradle with a resounding explosion in Mr. Smith's ear. Put it back gently as you would a baby. You can break the connection with one finger of your free hand pressing down the hook or the spring. Then you can reseat the receiver. Incidentally this is a good habit to acquire on closing all telephone conversations. It produces only a slight click, no explosion.

NOTE: See previous comment under Receiving Calls, (number *VI*, p. 100) about putting the receiver down gently if you have to look up information. The whole point is to have consideration for the other party's ear and sensibilities. You know how the crash of a receiver in your own ear affects your disposition.

Call-Backs: When leaving a message for Mr. Smith to call you back, in case you do not reach him on your first call, be sure to give your name, your number, and when you will be at your number. Don't dash out, or catch a plane. Mr. Smith will not be pleased when he calls back and learns that you have left and nobody knows when you will return.

The better procedure is to find out if you can when Mr. Smith will be in his office and then do the calling back yourself. You can always say: "This is Father Matthew from St. Patrick's Church. When do you expect Mr. Smith? Thank you, I'll call back then," or "I'll try to reach him later."

II. Long-Distance Calls

GENERAL

There are some very definite rules which you must observe in placing long distance calls. Some pastors are very exacting in this respect; others allow certain latitude in the matter. You must be governed, in general, by the accepted practice in your own rectory, but here are some specific suggestions which may avoid a breach with the pastor.

Before Calls:

1. Follow the custom of the rectory. Get permission where it is required *before* placing the call. In some cases casual or tacit permission is sufficient; in other cases a formal request is expected. Know your pastor and his methods of operation! You will soon learn whether you are expected to pay for your toll charges but make the gesture, at least, until a pattern has been established.

2. If you are a guest in another rectory do not presume permission to place a long distance call without explicit permission of the pastor.

During Calls:

1. Make your conversation, whether at your own rectory or when visiting, as brief as possible. If the business involved cannot be disposed of in the initial rate period (3 to 5 minutes), then it requires a letter or an appointment. In most cases the emergency has ceased to exist after three minutes or it requires more detailed study.

2. Do not use long distance calls for social visiting. Confine such calls to the business at hand.

After Calls:

1. If you are at home, put a slip in the pastor's mailbox, on his desk, or elsewhere, with the date, place, and time of the call, so he can check when the statement comes in from the telephone company.

2. If you are a visitor and have permission to place the toll call, it does not necessarily mean you are freed from paying for it. When you place the call, ask the operator to notify you of the charges when the call is terminated. Then leave a record slip with the exact amount reported by the operator. Whether your host accepts the payment or not is another matter. You will have observed the proprieties.

However, rather than requesting the operator for charges and paying your host, there is a simpler method which obviates any embarrassment: *You can ask the operator to have your call billed to your home telephone.*

3. If your toll call is to your own family residence which is out of town, the proper thing to do is to "reverse" the charges so that your pastor will not be obligated. Do not presume upon the pastor's good nature or generosity and run up a substantial toll bill on him for family calls. Use considered judgment.

How to Make Calls:

There are four types of long distance calls: (*A*) Station-to Station; (*B*) Person-to-Person; (*C*) Collect; (*D*) Direct Distance Dialing (*D.D.D.*)

A Type:

If you will talk to anybody who answers (*A* type) just tell the operator the town and telephone number you want. If you don't know the telephone number, give the operator the name and address and she will get it while you stay on the line. Charges start when the number is reached. If you are visiting be sure you know the number of the phone you are using. In many cases *A* type calls can be dialed direct and do not need the services of an operator. See *D* type below for details.

B Type:

If you want to reach a particular person by name or title, or extension, tell the operator when you place the call. Charges begin when the person or extension you want answers. *B* rates are higher than the *A* rates, but there is no charge if the person is not reached.

C Type:

If you want to reverse the charges, that is to call "collect" tell the operator so when you place the call. Charges do not begin until the called person accepts the charges.

In all cases remain on the telephone until the call is completed or until you receive a report.

If the connection cannot be made at the time of the call, then you may want to cancel the call and place it again later. However, if you request the operator to continue trying to complete it, remain near the telephone. If it is necessary for you to leave, make certain that someone near the telephone knows where you can be reached in the house. Otherwise, postpone the call.

It is inconsiderate on your part if you permit the operator to get the person you called on the line and then not be able to reach you because you have taken off elsewhere. If and when you are finally located, he won't be very well disposed toward you for having taken up his time thoughtlessly.

D Type:

1. This is the latest form of "direct distance dialing" called

by the telephone company *D.D.D.* It enables you to dial telephones in other cities by using a distant area code of three numbers (which are different from your own area code of three digits). Many area codes are now given in the front pages of your local telephone directory.

2. This method of distant calling does not involve the services of any telephone operator, although in some areas the operator will come in on the line and ask the number of the telephone you are using. The designated area code (of three numbers) is dialed first, then immediately the seven numbers (or two letters and five numbers) of the telephone (residence or business) you are calling.

3. The called party will answer as though receiving a local call. The toll charges start when the party called answers. The toll charges are recorded automatically on tape in the telephone office.

4. Your call will always go through faster if you use the area code when calling a telephone with a different area code. Check in the front of your telephone directory for the list of area codes.

The telephone company, in many cases, will supply you with a little blue book, upon application, containing a list of these area codes.

5. For more detailed information on this method of long distance calls, consult the front pages of your telephone directory. It will become the future popular method of immediate conversation anywhere in the United States, so become familiar with its methods.

Chapter 15. CORRESPONDENCE

Commentary

It is a lamentable fact that many of our young priests are notoriously neglectful and inconsiderate letter writers.

This dilatory habit may have been acquired in the seminary, where letter writing is limited, but efficiency in your ministry demands that it be corrected.

It cannot be emphasized too much that today, for many priests, letter writing has become almost a lost art. This is true, not only of the priest's parish and social correspondence, but also of his business letters.

Yet, oddly enough, the same priest who is a major offender in answering correspondence, may be unreasonably critical of those who do not immediately reply to his brusque notes. It is a two-way street, both lanes must be kept clear . . . incoming and outgoing.

The first rule, both of charity and of good manners, for your correspondence is, "Every letter that requires an answer should be answered promptly."

A very commendable resolution for you, the recently ordained priest, is the firm determination to answer every letter requiring an answer on the *same day* that you receive it.

This resolution should also apply to letters that pose a problem or ask for information which must be checked.

You should acknowledge receipt of the letter by return mail and inform the writer approximately when to expect a complete answer. This practice takes only a few minutes of your time, and it assures the original writer that his letter is receiving attention.

Challenge: If you, the newly assigned assistant, really wish to overcome your dillydallying and procrastination in answering your mail, here is a sure-fire method: Isolate your unanswered mail on your cluttered desk. Group it in a prominent place where it will always confront you — like a red signal. Resolve to reduce the pile each day. If you are in dead earnest, you will soon have the spot as bare as Mother Hubbard's cupboard! Keep it that way!

For the Seminarian

Some seminarians may be engaged in seminary publications, editorial work, etc. These duties may require business letters. The prescribed rules, in this chapter, for priests under "Business Letters," below, apply to these seminarians.

Keep in touch, of course, with your bishop, if you are not in his own seminary, your pastor, friends in other seminaries and convents. But most of your correspondence will be letters home, or to relatives. These are personal letters and they may be either typed or penned.

However, the letters home, out of love and respect for your family, should be at reasonably frequent intervals, according to the regulations of your particular seminary.

Your letters home should not be "duty" letters, but informative ones about your life and activities, displaying an interest in the affairs of the family and their home life. Try to visualize your parents or relatives and their interest in you. Then your letters to them will have the proper rapport.

Letters you receive from others concerning benefactions, invitations, announcements of births and deaths, etc., require prompt answers as an obligation of charity and of common propriety.

There are cards for all these occasions obtainable at most stationery stores and many of them are available in your own bookstore. Even if special cards are not in supply at your seminary, correspondence cards are, and they should be used, preferably with pen to give them the personal touch.

The detailed information on this subject — contained under "Personal Letters for the Priest" applies with proportionate force to you, the seminarian.

The major emphasis here is that every seminarian, at one time or another in his assignment as a diocesan priest, may have to carry on a correspondence as large as that of the average businessman, and all without benefit of secretary or stenographer.

The sooner you, as a seminarian, acquire the habit of promptness, neatness, brevity, and accuracy in your letters, the better prepared you will be for your future duties. It will require self-conquest and diligence, but it will return gratifying profits both to you and to the diocese.

For the Priest

The letters you will write as a priest are of two kinds:
1. Business
2. Personal

I. Business Letters

General Notes

All rectories furnish printed letterheads and envelopes. Most of them also have correspondence cards available.

Personalized name pads, usually intended for hasty notes of intercommunication within the diocese, are quite proper and practical, but they should be confined to that specific area.

This is not the place to detail the accepted rules for business typed letters, form, paragraphing, salutation, and signature. If you are in doubt on any of these points you can easily refresh your memory by a quick glance at any standard typewriting manual. Or if you have conveniently forgotten all that the diligent professors tried to teach you in this regard, then you need more than a "refresher" hypodermic. You will need to read and study some standard work on "Business Letters." For instance, *New Esquire Etiquette for Men* covers these points under the heading "Paperwork: Business Letters and Cards — looks, style and content." This review should supply your deficiency needs in vitamin capsule form. But, remember, there is no valid excuse for the priest not knowing the proprieties of letter writing. Use a dictionary for correct spelling, don't take chances.

Correct Forms

There are approved forms of ecclesiastical address, salutation, and conclusion to letters in use in the United States.

While there are some variations and flexibility in the official lists of some dioceses, for the most part these clergy forms follow a general pattern.

You, the seminarian, will ordinarily follow the approved forms of your particular diocese. However a complete chart is furnished here for letters you may write to all degrees of ecclesiastical rank, including religious superiors, brothers, and sisters.

If you are in any doubt as to the correct manner of address, the chart will furnish you with an approved form which you can use with confidence.

Suggestions for Business Letters

All business letters should be typed. Elite or pica type (small or large) is a matter of choice, but oddities in type, such as italics and small capitals, are not proper for normal business usage.

Answer all letters promptly, the same day if possible. Ten days, in the business world, is considered the maximum limit.

If you cannot answer fully within that period you certainly can acknowledge the letter within that time and explain your delay.

It is good manners to make your business letters as short as possible, but do not make them curt. There is a great difference between "conciseness" and "curtness." It is entirely possible to make a friendly letter concise. For example, do *not* say: "I have your letter of recent date," or "Yours of the 16th received and contents noted." Instead say, "Thank you for your letter of June 16th." This is much more courteous and exact. It will create a receptive mood when it is received.

This point needs to be emphasized. Saying something the nice way does not require elaborate phrasing, or long sentences, or "chitchat" that runs on and on. The pleasant letter takes only a few more words than the disagreeable one, and it gets better results.

In fact, it is as much a matter of attitude as it is of language. Be yourself, be natural, but be conscious that you are writing a letter, not carrying on a conversation.

If you forget all the above suggestions, just remember this one rule of four "C's." A good business letter is *Clear, Concise, Correct, Complete*.

But avoid that fifth "C" — *Curt*.

II. Personal Letters

General Notes

The extent and amount of your correspondence will depend in a large measure upon your personal disposition and inclination. But there are certain letters which you are definitely obliged to write by all the ordinary conventions of your clerical state.

Your letter writing will be composed of two classes:

A. Letters which you originate, and

B. Answers to letters received.

Both must be considered in detail.

A.   ORIGINATING LETTERS

Correspondence which you initiate will be of four types:

a) Personal

b) Congratulatory

c) Thank You

d) Special Occasions

a)   PERSONAL LETTERS

These are either personal-business which follow the rules of business correspondence as noted previously under "Business Letters," or they are social letters.

The social letters are informal. They may be typed or written in ink. The salutation and the close depend upon the degree of relationship or familiarity with the person addressed, but in all cases the signature must definitely be written in ink.

The content of the letter will be determined by its purpose, but make it a "communication" with your reader. Don't let "duty" barbs stick out in each paragraph to pierce the sensitivities of the reader. Make the letter a cordial visit. Let it be greeted with the same warmth as though you were at the front door in person.

b)   CONGRATULATIONS

These letters include birthdays, graduations, marriages, elections, promotions, appointments, congratulations, and the like.

Commercial cards are acceptable today for all these occasions. It is generally recognized that the busy priest cannot find time in his crowded schedule to write longhand letters for all these happenings.

A short written message, however, on the engraved or printed card personalizes it and carries more meaning to the recipient. This message and the signature should always be in ink.

The choice of the printed sentiment on the card should always be suitable to the particular occasion. Beware of "joke" cards that may be interpreted as offensive.

c)   THANK-YOU MESSAGES

Among the social imperatives are thank-you cards or letters. These include hospitality, bread-and-butter messages, thanks for presents, replies to expressions of good will and congratulations on any honors you may have received.

Commercial cards with envelopes are available for all these occasions, including "Thank You" cards. They can be obtained in a variety of forms, both religious and general, and their use, even if not extolled is better than no reply at all.

A hospitality card, or for that matter all other thank-you cards, should be sent not more than one week after you have accepted the hospitality or received the congratulatory message.

Whether you use a commercial card or a parish correspondence card, it should be sealed in an envelope (never a post card). It should contain some comment about why you enjoyed the visit so much, or some special remarks which personalize the message and take away any hint of mere formality.

The same is true when you write a thank-you note for any present or expression of good will. The rule is when anybody

writes you to congratulate you or for any other reason —
always write back. Such thank-you letters may be very short,
but they must contain the personal note. In a word, be liberal
with your thank-you notes, and you will never offend.

NOTE: One compelling reason for these "thank you" messages is that they are the only way the people who congratulate you, or send you presents, will know positively that you
received the message or gift. The measure of your appreciation (and your social conformity) will be judged by the
promptness of your acknowledgment.

d)   SPECIAL OCCASIONS

These letters include your Christmas and Easter greetings;
your congratulations on ordinations and jubilees; the religious
anniversaries of other priests or of sisters; and your apology
messages.

Here again commercial cards may be used for all except
apology letters.

If you have your Christmas or Easter cards printed, or if
the parish furnishes them, take the time and consideration to
write a short personal message and to hand-sign the cards.
This conveys the proper spirit of the season expected from a
priest and it takes away the "commercial" or "duty" aspect
of the greeting. Genuine feeling will inspire you what to say
on these personal messages. Be generous in sending cards to
your relatives, friends, the sick, etc.

The time you take to include the personal note on the
other special cards will more than repay you in the happiness
your special message will bring to the receiver.

Letters of apology should be treated "special." They should
be written notes on correspondence cards explaining the sudden failure to keep an appointment, or the circumstances that
prevented your appearance at a function, or any other failure

on your part. Such notes need not be too definite or detailed, but they indicate you did not forget the engagement but you were prevented from keeping it. But if it was a dinner engagement, Forty Hours, First Mass, etc., you had to miss, you are not excused from *telephoning* your inability to come.

B.   Answering Letters

You will be required to answer two types of letters:

a) Professional
b) Social

a)   professional replies

Under this heading are the letters which you receive in your capacity as a priest. These include Mass stipends, benefactions, invitations, condolence, and those which seek professional direction and information, or those which ask moral and doctrinal questions. All these you are definitely obliged to answer.

Your own instincts will prompt you as to the type of reply that is appropriate in the various circumstances. The Mass stipends, if sent to you personally, require a personal reply. This can, however, be on a thank-you card or a regular form provided in many of the parish rectories.

The other classifications, benefactions and invitations, will have to be answered according to the particular conditions in each case, but the reply should carry the personal note.

Acknowledgments of letters of condolence should be prompt, brief and personal. When someone has taken the trouble to write you a personal message of condolence, which is incidentally the most difficult kind of letter to write, he cannot but feel slapped if your thanks is impersonal.

It will be very little more trouble for you to write a line of thanks on plain notepaper, letterhead, or correspondence card than to address a boxful of expensive and meaningless form cards. If, however, you do use the prevalent standard forms, be sure you include the written line of thanks on it. Make it personal. Remember the letter you received was personal.

Letters seeking information or asking questions should be answered promptly and as thoroughly as possible. Such letters may be typed, for they are businesslike replies. Just remember that the letter represents you and your priesthood. If you cannot give a complete answer immediately, send a short courteous note that the inquiry has been received and you are gathering the information or referring it to the proper sources for a thorough reply.

b)   SOCIAL REPLIES

When you answer letters from home, relatives, or friends, let the letter be the type which makes their faces light up when they recognize from the envelope that it is a message from you.

The contents of the letter should reflect your personality and your interests. Letter writing under these conditions is not an art, but an outpouring of yourself.

There should be much of "you" in the letter and the words will tumble magically from the typewriter. There should be a lot about "us" in the typed sheet — the folks at home — your pleasure about something we have done, or are planning to do, our activities.

In other words, you do not need any rules for answering these letters. They will be the closest substitute to a personal visit. You will not be concerned about form but will be absorbed in content. These are the letters everyone likes to receive, especially the folks at home.

ECCLESIASTICAL FORMS FOR USE BY SEMINARIANS

Name	Envelope and Letter
Pope	His Holiness, Pope John XXIII Vatican City *Salutation* *Close* Your Holiness: Your dutiful son,
Cardinal	His Eminence Albert Cardinal Meyer Archbishop of Chicago 1555 North State Street Chicago 10, Illinois NOTE: Some dioceses, notably Boston, omit "His Eminence." *Salutation* *Close* Your Eminence: Respectfully yours in Christ,
Archbishop	The Most Reverend Paul J. Jones, D.D. Archbishop of Winchester 55 Evergreen Avenue Winchester 12, Minnesota *Salutation* *Close* Your Excellency: Respectfully yours in Christ,
Bishop	The Most Reverend John D. Ward, D.D. Bishop of Melrose 4525 Long Avenue Melrose 10, Nebraska *Salutation* *Close* Your Excellency: Respectfully yours in Christ,
Domestic Prelate	The Right Reverend Monsignor Francis A. Murray[1] 5957 West Orange Boulevard Santa Caterina, California NOTE: Some dioceses, notably Boston, omit "Monsignor." *Salutation* *Close* Right Reverend and Respectfully yours in Christ, Dear Monsignor, or Dear Monsignor Murray:[2]
Papal Chamberlain	The Very Reverend Monsignor Paul T. Brown[1] St. Monica's Rectory 1456 West Walnut Street Milwaukee 3, Wisconsin NOTE: Some dioceses, notably Boston, omit "Monsignor." *Salutation* *Close* Very Reverend and Respectfully yours in Christ, Dear Monsignor, or Dear Monsignor Brown:[2]

[1] Add: P.A. if Prothonotary Apostolic
        P.P. if Permanent Pastor
        V.F. if Rural Dean
[2] These informal titles are used according to the degree of relationship.

Name	Envelope and Letter
Rector of Seminary	The Very Reverend Paul J. Lane, Rector St. Damian's Seminary 1500 Ashley Road St. Petersburg, Florida <small>(If the Rector is a Domestic Prelate or a Papal Chamberlain, address him as noted for these titles.)</small> *Salutation* *Close* Dear Father Rector: Respectfully yours in Christ,
Rural Dean	The Very Reverend John Beck, V.F. St. Jerome's Rectory Smithfield, Indiana *Salutation* *Close* Dear Reverend Dean: Respectfully yours in Christ,
Diocesan Priest	The Reverend Carl M. Bauer, Pastor St. Boniface Rectory 2610 Hartford Road Hagerstown, Maryland *Salutation* *Close* Dear Father: Respectfully yours in Christ,
Clerics in Major Orders	The Reverend Mr. James F. Faber St. James Seminary 1000 Meridian Avenue Bloomingdale, Utah *Salutation* *Close* Dear Reverend Sir, or Respectfully yours in Christ, or Dear James:[2] Cordially yours,[2]
Seminarian	Mr. James E. Block Mount Saint Mary Seminary Greenville, Kentucky *Salutation* *Close* Dear Mr. Block, or Respectfully yours in Christ, or Dear James:[2] Cordially yours,[2]

PROPER FORMS FOR RELIGIOUS (MEN & WOMEN)

Name	Envelope and Letter
Abbot	The Right Reverend Ambrose Goldrick, O.S.B.[3] St. Procopius Abbey Lisle, Illinois *Salutation* *Close* Dear Father Abbot: Respectfully yours in St. Benedict[4]

[3] Use letters proper to his (or her) religious group. A complete list of abbreviations will be found in the *Catholic Directory* under the title "Index for Statistics of Religious Orders" for the various organizations of religious priests, Brothers, and Sisters.
[4] Use name of the religious founder or patron.

Name	Envelope and Letter
Provincial	The Very Reverend John J. Block, O.P.[3] Provincial Holy Name Province 1360 South Park Drive Washburn, Ohio *Salutation* *Close* Dear Father Provincial: Respectfully yours in St. Dominic,[4]
Prior	The Very Reverend George B. Trumble,[3] Prior Carmelite Priory of St. Cyril Rochester 9, New York *Salutation* *Close* Dear Father Prior: Respectfully yours in — [4]
Mother Superior	The Reverend Mother Mary Joseph[3] Motherhouse of the Sacred Heart 876 Woodridge Drive Doschester, Iowa *Salutation* *Close* Dear Reverend Mother, or Respectfully yours in — [4] Reverend Mother:
Religious Priest	The Very Reverend John K. Walter,[3] or The Reverend John K. Walter[3] (According to rank or dignity, consult *Catholic Directory*.) *Salutation* *Close* Dear Father Walter: Respectfully yours in — [4]
Brother	Brother Reginald[3] (Add title to name if any, e.g., "Superior" or "Principal.") *Salutation* *Close* Dear Brother: Respectfully yours in — [4] or Fraternally yours,
Sister	Sister Mary Thomasine, C.J.C.[3] (Add title to name if any, e.g., "Superior" or "Principal.") *Salutation* *Close* Dear Mother, or Respectfully yours in — [4] or Dear Sister: Fraternally yours, Note: Some communities title the Superior "Reverend Mother," e.g., Reverend Mother Mary Thomasine. Some communities use the title "Mother" for all its members, instead of "Sister." Consult *Catholic Directory*, if in doubt.

Chapter 16. INTRODUCTIONS

Timid Approach

The matter of propriety in introductions gives much concern to the seminarian and young priest. When you are confronted with an actual situation, especially if you encounter it unexpectedly, such as introducing your bishop to another, presenting your classmates to your parents, introducing two ladies to each other, you will probably flounder around in a daze, and stammer out some incoherent jumble.

Calm yourself! There is a simple safeguard: Just remember two simple rules for general introductions and one special one for clerics and dignitaries. First let's consider the two regular rules to be fixed firmly in your memory.

Here is an important hint: if you forget the more formidable word *introduction* and substitute the simpler one *present* much of your confusion will clear up.

First Rule of Introductions

To the woman always present the man.

The above is admittedly an awkward sentence, but the woman must be mentioned *first,* "Mrs. Prima, this is Mr. Secundus" or simply "Mrs. Smith, Mr. Brown."

Today introductions (presentations) have become that plain and simple, "Mrs. Smith, Mr. Brown." In this age of rocket speed the old forms are rapidly becoming obsolete. "May I present?" or "May I introduce?" or "I have the honor to present" — all these stilted phrases, while formally correct, are too stiff and slow-paced for modern usage.

Remembering the simple rule, "Mrs. Prima, Mr. Secundus" you will easily avoid the bad forms . . . maybe they shouldn't even be mentioned . . . such as, "Shake hands with" or "Meet Mr. Brown" or "Make the acquaintance of Mr. Brown." Don't be caught with them anywhere — they are bad company!

Today it is (to repeat for emphasis) "Mrs. Smith, Mr. Brown." That is all you have to do to present a man to a woman. Just mention the two names, always with "Ladies first." What could be simpler or easier for you to remember?

Just be sure that you enunciate both names clearly and distinctly so that both people will understand them. Then your job is done. The rest is in their hands.

Presenting the Family

It is best for you, as a prospective priest, to avoid first name presentations, except with your immediate family. "Mother, this is Mr. Brown." "Mary, this is Mr. Brown — my sister." "George, this is Mr. Brown — my brother."

Presenting a Group

When more than two people are involved in your presentation, do not let the situation confuse you. It is really very simple. Forget about rank or form or sex (for the moment). Merely mention the newcomer's name, "Mr. Brown," then the names of the others in the group in the order in which they happen to be standing or sitting at the time. "Mr. Brown, Mr. Smith, Mrs. Jones, Miss Jackson, Mr. Black."

If the group is larger or inattentive, a general introduction is not necessary. Just present Mr. Brown to the two or three persons nearest to you and let the matter take care of itself from there on.

Second Rule of Introductions

The honored one's name is always said first. "Mr. Primus, Mr. Secundus."

If you remember your first rule: "Ladies first" you won't have any trouble with this second one: "Important name first." However, don't struggle with the fine distinctions, just introduce them. Your instincts will tell you to mention the more important name first. "Professor Yale, this is my brother, Jim." "Mother, this is my roommate, Frank Hanley."

By the book you should present the young to the old, the man to the woman, the boy to the girl, the lesser to the greater, but you run into difficulties when you present a man to a man, or a woman to a woman. How are you going to appraise the age of woman, or the importance of men? Don't court trouble!

Safe Method

The secret of the procedure is to follow your instincts as to the name mentioned first and then be sure to say both names clearly and in the same tone of voice, giving no more importance to one than to the other. "Mrs. Smith, Mrs. Jones."

With this short form, nobody will really notice or care if you miss a fine distinction of seniority or importance. Again, just introduce them in the same tone of voice and let them pick it up from there. "Mr. Thomas, Mr. Brown."

Third Rule of Introductions

Here we have the exceptions for clergy and officials which you as a priest will encounter in making introductions.

The general rule still holds: mention the name of the senior first: "Monsignor Daley, Father Burns."

The exceptions arise in the presentation to Church prelates

and clergymen, public executives and officials. These exceptions impose some restrictions on the "Ladies first," and there is a sharp distinction between the accepted formula for men and that for women. It will be necessary to consider them in their respective order.

I. Presentation of Men to Clergy

You may seldom be called on to present anyone to a cardinal or a bishop, but you will frequently introduce a monsignor or your pastor.

The general rule holds: Mention the name of the dignitary first and present the clergyman or the layman to him. "Monsignor Daley, this is my father, Mr. Hopkins."

THE CORRECT TITLE

The proper salutation for these various ranks in dignity is definitely fixed. They are:

Rank	Address
Cardinal	Your Eminence
Archbishop (Bishop)	Your Excellency
Monsignor (All)	Monsignor
Priests (All)	Father

You follow the regular simple form: "Your Eminence, Father Jones, my classmate." or "Your Excellency, my father, Mr. Hopkins."

All bishops are addressed "Your Excellency" and the same formula is used for all of them, archbishops, bishops, auxiliaries.

When you present anyone to a monsignor or to another priest, you may shade the formality somewhat and say "Monsignor, this is Father Jones, a classmate," or "Father Smith, this is my brother, Frank."

When you introduce priests to each other, you are on common ground and you say, "Father Smith, Father Jones." Here it isn't so important which name you mention first unless one is obviously the senior in service or dignity. Then accord him the distinction of being mentioned first. But this point does not have to be labored. You will do it almost intuitively.

You can ease the awkward pause which may follow the introduction by a brief supplementary sentence. "Father Smith is from the seminary, Father Jones is on the mission band." Then let the two priests pick it up from there.

II.   Presentation of Women to Clergy

Here is one place where the women gracefully relinquish their first place.

A woman is always presented to a cardinal, a bishop, or a monsignor, and it is not incorrect to present her to a priest.

The correct form is, "Your Eminence (or your Excellency), Mrs. Thomas."

For the monsignor you mention his name, "Monsignor Curley, Mrs. Thomas."

This simplified form is rapidly replacing the more formal "Your Excellency (or Monsignor), may I present Mrs. Thomas?" The reason for the change is obvious: introductions (or presentations) are no longer stilted. They are simple and unaffected. Nobody will note the *form* of your presentation if your *manner* is gracious.

ANENT PRIESTS

In the case of priests it is not incorrect to present the women to them and this rule may be safely followed, but a subtle distinction enters in this area — you have to be guided by circumstances and seniority. But, again, your own sense of fitness will direct you. However, you stand for all introductions, as do all men being introduced.

Here are a few illustrations. If the priest is a veteran in the service, it is a nice gesture to present your mother (or any other woman) to him.

If he is your pastor or one of your professors, you should present your relatives to him. "Father Murphy, this is my aunt, Mrs. Sawyer."

If you are on the same seniority level as the priest, or if he is a close associate, you can quite properly present him with "Mother, this is Father Horan, you have heard me speak of him. We are classmates" or whatever fits the circumstances.

But in any situation do not be unduly disturbed about the form. If your manner is gracious nobody will be critical, or even notice the method used.

III. Presentation to Public Executives and Officials

Here again the standard rules apply. The more honorable name is mentioned first and you present your relatives or friends to him, addressing the honorable one by his official title. "Mr. President," "Senator Hanagan," "Mr. White" (for a Congressman), "Mayor Daley," or "Mr. Mayor," "Judge White," "Doctor Nash" — and so on through the official list.

You present all your male relatives or friends to them. "Mr. Mayor (or Mayor Daley, my father, Mr. Williams." However, it is "Ladies First" with a few exceptions. You say "Mother, Judge Sewalocki, my mother, Mrs. Williams." You add that appendix "My mother, Mrs. Williams" to save the Judge any embarrassment about names, for undoubtedly he meets many people and might be lost for the moment as to your family name.

You probably won't ever encounter the exceptions for women, but it is well to know them. Here they are: You present the woman to the President, to any member of a reigning family and to a foreign ambassador.

You can forget about the last two — royalty and ambassador — but if you are ever lucky enough to introduce your mother, sister, or aunt to our President, the form is, "Mr. President, I have the honor to present my mother, Mrs. Hamilton." In this stately situation the formal presentation is still the practice.

PRIEST TO PRIEST

Here is a situation the seminarian and the young priest will meet frequently at seminary functions, ordinations, parish church celebrations — wherever the clergy gather for church services.

While vesting in the rectory or sacristy, during the procession, after services, in the social hour following the affair, in any of these situations older priests may introduce themselves to you. The veteran will simply say, "I'm Father (or Frank) Jones" and extend his hand. The younger priest replies in kind: "I'm Fred Stone."

The young priest will shake hands and acknowledge the greeting, but — and here comes the rub — it seems that almost invariably the young priest will fail to mention his own name. The older priest who was fraternal enough to introduce himself is then placed in the awkward position of being compelled to say, "And what is your name, Father?"

Don't you, the young priest, be guilty of this execrable fault. Make a mental note now, as you read this, to always give your name clearly and distinctly to the priest who was gracious enough to introduce himself in the first place.

This same routine will hold when you are in your own rectory, only this time you must take the initiative. If the pastor has a priest guest in the house, or in the living room, and you come upon him for the first time, it is your obligation to introduce yourself to him, "I'm Father White, the assistant." You can be assured that the guest priest will know how to pick it up from there.

The same procedure is followed if you should answer the doorbell and a priest is standing there. You do not question him, but hold the door open for him and introduce yourself, "I'm Father White, the assistant," then respectfully await developments.

This mentioning of your own name must also be remembered when some layman introduces himself to you, at a sports event, in an airport, wherever people meet in public. It is a friendly gesture on the part of the layman and you should respond with equal affability. Speak your name clearly. If it is a difficult one — all the more reason for you to be articulate.

When YOU Are Presented

Now on the other side of the coin, how should *you* act when *you* are introduced?

To a Prelate

If you are presented to a cardinal or a bishop, you extend your right hand. The prelate puts his right hand in yours. You bend your knee and kiss his ring.

NOTE: Strictly speaking according to the social authorities, you genuflect — and that on the *left* knee — only when meeting your ordinary within your own diocese when you kiss his ring. But practice is becoming more extensive in this regard, so it is not improper to make the genuflection to any bishop you meet. Also, it is awkward for you to genuflect on the left knee, since you are accustomed to using the right knee, so most people are using the right knee.

Some bishops have a little trick of grasping your hand in such a manner that it indicates they do not wish you to bend your knee. You will catch on quickly. It is the kissing of the ring that is indulgenced.

To a Man

First of all you stand whether being introduced to a man or woman. Then you say, "How do you do," but don't make a question out of it by using a rising inflection. It does not require an answer.

You may repeat the newly met person's name if you like (and it is a good thing to do so to fix it in your memory), but never acknowledge the introduction with just a curt "Mr. Simpson." Instead say, "How do you do, Mr. Simpson."

You shake hands with Mr. Simpson, and no matter how bored you are about the whole situation, don't take it out on Mr. Simpson. Maybe he feels the same way about it, but match his smile and cordiality.

An Important Warning: When you shake hands with Mr. Simpson, do not give him an exhibition of your strength by squeezing his hand as though it is caught in a vise. The poor fellow may have arthritis and may be just getting the circulation back after his recent encounter with your classmate and his athletic prowess. If you give Mr. Simpson a championship handshake he will long remember you, but not pleasantly. Give him a firm grasp but omit the extra pressure.

To a Woman

To Mrs. Simpson, you give a courteous nod, but you do not offer your hand, unless she first offers hers, which she will probably do to a priest. But, again, don't make her regret that she did so by your painful pressure.

On the Street

If the introduction to a man takes place outdoors and your hands are gloved, as in winter street wear, you do not remove the right glove, nor do you say "Please excuse my glove." This remark is falling into disuse because of the obviousness of the situation — a handshake can't wait until you peel off the glove, and the glove is proper attire for street wear, so why call attention to a normal situation?

If the man raises his hat to you, as he will probably do, you return the courtesy.

Meeting the Ladies

In the case of a lady being introduced to you on the street you raise your hat and acknowledge the introduction, but you do not offer to shake hands unless she first offers to do so. Then you can follow the above method for the glove routine.

Conclusion

If in reading this section you are inclined to scoff at all these detailed regulations, just read the following excerpt.

Very Reverend Francis J. Connell, C.Ss.R., Catholic University, Washington, D. C., has this to say about introductions and courtesy toward others in his little pamphlet, "The Gentlemanly Priest."

> Courtesy demands that the priest learn and use the titles proper to dignitaries of church and state. It is essential for a gentleman to be a gentle man. The priest's kindness must be universal in its scope.

> The priest who is courteous and suave towards the exquisite members of the young ladies' sodality but grouchy and querulous towards the old housekeeper whose charms have long since departed does not show himself a very apt pupil in learning the meekness of his Divine Master.

However, in his dealing with others the priest can *fail* by excessive obsequiousness as well as by lack of respect. There is nothing praiseworthy from the standpoint of humility or obedience or courtesy in a bearing that betokens extreme timidity. There is no reason why the priest, elevated as he is by his sacred office, should become frightened and nonplussed when he is in the company of some eminent personage.

The truth of the matter is that the truly great are very simple and unassuming, and wish to be treated *without* excessive marks of deference. It is only the man who lacks genuine greatness of soul that is constantly solicitous that others do not forget the position he happens to have attained in civil or ecclesiastical circles.

So govern yourself accordingly.

Chapter 17. GOOD MANNERS IN ACTION

General

The conduct proposed in this chapter offers you an opportunity to practice good manners in many concrete ways.

The list is by no means exhaustive. It is merely exploratory of some specific ways in which you can put what you have learned, by reading this book, into your practical everyday seminary life. It is, as it were, an examination of conscience, whereby you may see wherein you can improve your exemplification of Christian charity toward your fellow seminarians, and also to survey how you can improve your own actions, so as to advance on the road to Christian perfection.

No effort has been made to "prove-in" these questions. They are classified in their surroundings, where they operate, and it is easy for you to make subjective analysis when you are in that particular environment. Just ask yourself the question: How do I score in this test? Can I answer "Yes" to all these questions? If you can do so you rate an "A." If not, then mark yourself accordingly, with a resolution to improve in the deficiency ratings.

In the Sacristy

Dress: Do I pass inspection as to hands, fingernails, hair, white shirt, surplice, and cassock — are all in good order?

Rules: Do I remember that silence is golden? Do I keep

dignified silence during rehearsal in sacristy and sanctuary? Do I refrain from chitchat with other seminarians or servers?

Promptness: Am I on time for assignments so that the priest and community are not kept waiting?

Conduct: Do I observe the proprieties of saying "Good Morning" to the priest? Do I assist him with his coat if necessary? Do I help him with the vestments? Do I have altar and candles ready?

If other Masses are in progress while I am waiting, do I observe reverence by kneeling at the Consecration, Communion, and Blessing?

Am I exact in the observance of the rubrics, ceremonies, and Latin of the Mass? Have I learned the proper use of hands, holding of cruets, signs of the cross, genuflections, etc.?

In the Chapel

Do I kneel up straight in chapel? Sit erect? Keep feet on floor? Refrain from looking around?

Do I receive Holy Communion properly? That is, with eyes closed? Head back? Mouth opened properly and tongue well extended?

(NOTE: Later on you will be training children in proper behavior in this respect, so learn well yourself.)

Waiting on Table

Do I pass inspection as to: hands, fingernails, hair, clean shirt, well-pressed trousers, white coat (or apron)?

Do I observe the technique of serving food and removing dishes? Pouring coffee? Am I always ready for emergencies? Always on time? Quick to anticipate the wishes of the diners?

Do I observe silence? Refrain from "whistling while I work"?

Do I guard against: Clattering dishes? Slopping food?

Dropping dishes or silverware? Appropriating food not permitted to me? Rushing through the job as an unwelcome task . . . to be finished as quickly as possible?

In the Classroom

Do I realize that clock watching, or wristwatch inspection, is an open affront to the professor? Do I restrain such impulses?

Do I repress the urge to shuffle, stretch, or yawn during class? Do I realize that if I don't smother the inclination it will be a visible message to the professor (and to my classmates) that I am bored?

Am I inclined, half-consciously, to moan and groan aloud over the announcements the professor makes? If so, do I control the impulse and keep my insurgence to myself?

Do I sit up straight in class? Do I control the flash to kick the seat in front of me in order to register my disapproval?

Do I always address the professor as "Father"?

Do I realize that I will build up discontent in the class by complaining about the professor, his methods, his temperament, his idiosyncrasies, if he has any? Do I ever think ahead: "Some day I may be in his place, looking out on other students?"

Do I on written tests fill my paper with lots of slang, ungrammatical expressions, irrelevant matter, misspelled words? Am I foolish enough to think the professor will be dazzled by my loquaciousness? Or that he will ignore my attitude, or my assumed erudition?

In Sports

Am I a true sportsman under all circumstances? If you can't answer that question affirmatively, then give yourself this detailed test:

Do I wish to win the game by any and every shady means possible? Is winning my sole motivation?

Do I expect breaks myself, but never give them to others? Do I do anything to help the unskilled player acquire technique? Or am I a curmudgeon with my skill?

Do I rush out on the gym floor, or the athletic field, to protest angrily the decision of the official?

Do I berate the officials in front of team and spectators, at summer camp, or when I am coaching a team?

Do I lose sight of the "spiritual direction" of my team when I give vent to such verbal barrage on the officials?

Do I try to be a good sport in losing, and a modest hero in winning?

During Recreation

Here are a few pointers for recreation, and at other times. These are not put in question form, but given as admonitions.

However, if you wish to examine yourself critically on these items, you can "score" yourself privately on your rating.

Display some animation during this period. Do not be spongelike, absorbing everything. Be a "doer" contributing something.

Add something to the conversation, if it is only to raise the tone from that of a critical note to one of laudation.

Don't build up a private "clique." Talk to everybody (who will listen to you). Listen to everybody who wants to talk, even though it bores you.

Don't walk with just a few favored friends, but make companions of all. Of course, you like some better than others, that is natural. But remember recreation, talks and walks, sports and discussions are for all. They are common exercises; make your part in them general, not confined to a few select intimates.

Beware of pranks and "practical" jokes. They can be harmful and they can wound seriously. Have your fun, but if you want to make someone the butt of your jokes, make the victim yourself. Then you won't hurt anybody.

At Other Times

Here are a few suggestions for practicing charity and gaining Christian virtue.

Help slow students with their studies. If you are a near-genius, use the talents God has given you to help the less endowed. But do it quietly and privately.

Take corrections, from faculty or classmates, as a man. Don't resent them, don't sulk, don't be a crybaby.

Share your visitors with others who may not be so fortunate.

Don't be selfish or greedy, either at the table or in your room. Here is an example. It is not only bad manners, but it shows the selfish streak, if you take linens, blankets, furnishings from the supply rooms or from vacant rooms. Your selfishness is showing! If you need any new equipment, or you want to borrow any temporarily, such as floor polishers or vacuum cleaners, the one simple and polite way is for you to ask for it.

Don't be a kill-joy. Just because you are an upperclassman, don't picture to the younger seminarians the hard road ahead; the heavy load; the difficult years; the terrible grind. You may be a prophet of doom, but it doesn't follow that he is. He may enjoy the very work you found so difficult. He may like camp, for instance, which you didn't; he may be good in sports, which you disliked.

Let him live his own happy life with his own rosy outlook. Be a man!

Chapter 18. YOUR FIRST SOLEMN MASS

Your Goal Achieved

All your years of study, your spiritual development, your social training find their culmination in your First Solemn Mass. You return to your native parish, to your former grade school, to your relatives and friends as a priest of God.

It is a day of celebration for the entire congregation, a time of thanksgiving for your relatives, a humbling experience for you when you ascend the altar "a priest forever."

You have practiced the rubrics of the Mass for many days. You are letter perfect in all the ceremonies and the prayers. Your ministers are seasoned veterans. You need not agitate yourself too much over the church services. They will be performed properly. But there are other details which will concern you.

Guiding Principles

In any preparations you (or your family) may contemplate for your First Mass, the essential consideration must be the rigid observance of all regulations your bishop may have designated for such occasions, as well as strict compliance with any restrictions he may have placed upon the accompanying social celebrations.

It will be easy for you to familiarize yourself before ordination with such regulations by consulting your former associates who were ordained a year or two before you. Probably some tradition exists in your seminary regarding

these matters. If any doubt arises as to the propriety of any church or social observance, clear the doubt with your pastor before proceeding with your arrangements.

Other Details

There are, however, many other details of the day and the events leading up to it which must be planned in advance by you and your relatives. These particulars are enumerated here and directed to your attention in some detail, for you will be on retreat immediately before ordination and absorbed with many last minute sacerdotal preparations. You cannot be called into consultation at that time. Thus the purpose of this chapter is to specify the major details concerning your First Mass, and the mode of procedure regarding them, as they affect you, so that you may plan rationally before the final retreat.

General

There are many variants to First Mass celebrations. Much of the detailed observance depends upon extraneous circumstances. For instance, the place: a large parish in a big city, a suburban district, a country church — the details vary greatly in these given circumstances. Other factors that affect the celebration are whether First Masses are fairly regular in the church or whether it is an extraordinary event. Also to be considered are the social status and affluence of your immediate family, their acquaintance with the present pastor and with the members of the congregation.

These, and many other diverse factors determine the size and extent of the social observance of the event. Only the general rules can be mentioned here. They will have to be adjusted to the special circumstances surrounding your particular celebration.

Caution

It is well, however, to emphasize one caution here.

In preparation for the First Mass, and the incidental observance, it must be stressed that the central celebration is a spiritual one, the Solemn Mass itself. All other functions, decorations, church ornaments, flowers, singing, etc., should be subordinate to the Mass itself.

For instance, aisle carpets, sidewalk canopy, festoons on pews, these and similar decorations (and formal dress for male relatives or ushers) are quite proper for wedding ceremonies where the attention is centered on the bride, but they are not appropriate for First Masses where the Sacrifice of the Altar by the newly ordained priest is the essential element. There is also the matter of photographers. In some churches and at some weddings they swarm all over the sanctuary with flashing bulbs at every action. This is not proper for a First Mass. Moreover the pastor of the church may have his own definite regulations regarding the matter of photography.

Just remember that there is a fitting congruity or balance between the essentials and the incidentals which must not be disturbed. For instance, a small church, or a modernistic altar, can be overdecorated by a simple floral arrangement which would be lost in a large church, or on a gothic altar.

The prudent method in this regard, irrespective of who furnishes the decorations, is to be guided by the pastor's advice or by the officers of the Altar Society who are experienced in this matter.

The Remote Preparation

The church arrangements and the predetermined general plan of entertainment and hospitality must be made well in advance. Common sense dictates that the overall financial outlay be proportionate to the family's social status and to its pecuniary resources.

Here again there is a nicely balanced distinction between what is correct and suitable under the given conditions and what is pretentious and incongruous. Guests are quick to distinguish the genuine from the ostentatious. Keep in your own orbit and make your festive plans accordingly. This general overall policy should be clearly understood in the family circle before any definite commitments are made.

The Proximate Preparation

The first immediate preparation must be made with your pastor. Much depends upon the degree of your relationship with him. If he has sponsored you, or followed your progress in the clerical state, these arrangements will be easy and informal. But if your family has moved into another parish, or city, you may wish your First Mass in the old parish or elsewhere. Then, tact will be required on your part in dealing with the two pastors.

If you are not well acquainted with the pastor your meeting with him may be more formal and impersonal. But it should take place preferably well before your ordination date, but at the latest, on your last visit home as a deacon.

You must remember that it is his church, altar, choir, altar boys, ushers, congregation. You are requesting the use of his resources and his church for your special occasion. He may have his own ideas regarding the hour of your First Mass and the length of your special services, especially if another scheduled Mass follows your First Mass.

You must keep in mind that if a tight schedule exists in the church services, the length of the sermon for your Mass may disrupt the regular program. Advise your preacher in advance of the situation and the time element. You must also remember to allow time for your First Blessing (and the imparting of the Papal Blessing, if you are empowered to give it) and the egress of the people. You will probably find your pastor agreeable to all your reasonable proposals, but if an impasse develops you must conform to the pastor's decision.

The Choir

You will probably find your pastor readily agreeable to all your proposals. The problem of the choir, however, or the singing may be a precarious matter. The pastor or the choir director or the choir members may resent the importation of special soloists, or choristers, or organist for the occasion if you make this proposal. If there is any feeling in the matter you should not make a major issue of it. Keep things in proper perspective and maintain your tranquillity. The Mass itself is the major event. It will be remembered long after the singing is forgotten. So be on your guard against stirring up a hornet's nest.

Circumstances Vary

The pastor may have his own ideas on the matter of procession, first blessing and clergy breakfast in the rectory, following the Mass. He may have his thoughts on a parish reception in the church hall, a parish dinner in the school building. Or if it is a large city parish, First Masses may be an annual event to him and he may be too busy to give your celebration any special consideration.

On the other hand if you live in the suburbs or the country a First Mass may be an unusual event. The pastor may wish to make it a red-letter day with much solemnity and display.

The Pastor Consulted

These details must be worked out with the pastor in person (not by letter). Once you have reached agreement on the essential details, the family plans for dinner, reception, etc., can be dovetailed into the major program as determined by your interview with the pastor.

Incidentally this interview should also diplomatically establish the official function you wish the pastor to perform at your First Mass. If you wish to select your own ministers and preacher from among your classmates or professors, it is always a courteous request to ask the pastor to be the archpriest.

He will, then, not feel that he has been overlooked or left out of the scene in his own church. Much depends upon the degree of your relationship with the pastor and his own personal temperament. In any event do not wound his sensibilities.

Clerical Guests

The out-of-town clerical guests who are to assist at your First Mass are *your* guests and your responsibility. The pastor is under no obligation to lodge them, although if he has available space he may graciously offer to do so.

You probably already know the capacity of the parish rectory, so do not let any embarrassing situation arise. You can inform the pastor what arrangements you have made for their lodging — preferably at a hotel (where previous reservations have been secured in your name with the specification that you will honor all charges).

It will then be easy for you to determine the pastor's wishes regarding the visitors' Masses — whether he wishes them to say public Masses in the Church, or private Masses at the convent, on the side altars, or elsewhere. This way the house-keeper will know how many to expect for breakfast and will be prepared.

The Invitations

Once the actual date of your ordination is set, your parents should think about invitations. In all probability they already have a tentative list made up, but now it can be completed. This is one of the tasks that devolves on your parents, or your immediate relatives if your parents are deceased.

This is not the place to detail the obligations and conventional forms and practices for the parents, relatives, and their guests. Here we are concerned exclusively with those matters which pertain to you, the newly ordained priest.

Parents and relatives will find all the church and home etiquette, the reception, seating arrangements, costumes, sample invitations, menus, etc., amply covered in Mrs. Kay Toy Fenner's *American Catholic Etiquette* under the chapter "Holy Orders." This chapter covers in detail the parents' activity and etiquette for the ordination and the First Mass.

A Reminder

There is only one reminder for you, the ordained, before the invitations are sent out: make sure that your parents have your special list of friends *you* wish invited. And be sure to include on your list the Sisters and the lay teachers who taught you in grade school or elsewhere. They are so often forgotten, and you, perhaps, like so many other priests owe much to them for planting the seeds of vocation in your early schooldays. If you don't know the present address of a particular Sister, send the invitation to the parish school or motherhouse. It will be forwarded.

The Reception or Dinner

In some dioceses there are definite regulations (or approved practices) regarding receptions and public dinners for First Masses.

If your parents, or an organization, are contemplating such a social event, the first thing to do is to clear the matter with the pastor.

Then, you, the honored guest, need not concern yourself about the details of the arrangements, for those in charge will be fully competent to manage the affair.

Your only concern here is to make doubly sure that the pastor and the curates are formally invited — a detail which is sometimes neglected.

You may also express your wishes that the dinner (if one be given) start at the specified time; that no liquor be served; that there be a minimum of speeches. The whole emphasis here is that the social observance must not overshadow the spiritual significance of the event — the First Mass, and the church services.

Publicity

One detail on which many newly ordained priests fail is in proper newspaper publicity of the First Mass. This applies both to the Catholic and the daily press. And there is no good reason for this failure. It arises, in large part, from a lack of technical knowledge of the proper procedure. A First Mass is *news* and the papers are glad to have it, but you must take it to them. Just keep in mind a few simple rules.

The amount of space (coverage) you will receive from the daily press will be proportionate to its circulation. In a large city you will receive small notices. In a suburban or country place you will receive much more space, for it is important news to the limited number of subscribers of the local paper.

Your diocesan Catholic paper will probably cover your class ordination, with names, pictures, and places of First Masses. This information is usually supplied by the seminary with your assistance. But, if you sing your First Mass outside the diocese you should furnish the Catholic paper of the area with the pertinent information and a photo.

Preparing the Story

Your publicity should be prepared in advance, as soon as you have the details completed. If there are several newspapers in your city you should send a copy of the story to each newspaper together with accompanying photos. The story may be the same for all the papers with a release date on it. The papers will do their own editing of the story.

The copy you send the newspapers should be typed and double spaced. It should be composed in regular newspaper style, so that the facts are told in the first paragraph. The rest are the details — important ones first, minor ones toward the end. Thus the rewrite man in the newspaper office can delete the details as much as he wishes to fit the available space and yet have a complete story of facts. If you are in any doubt about the composition of your story, consult some of the articles written in the local and Catholic press of former First Masses.

Obtaining the Pictures

The photographs are a different matter. They must be unmounted glossy prints with your name typed out on a slip of paper attached with scotch tape to the back of the picture. Do not write on the back of a photograph; the impression will show upon the reproduction. You should send different studies, or poses, to the various papers, but this is not imperative. All of the pictures should be bust size, that is, "studio photo."

It will be easy for you to secure different poses. Your photographer will probably take several exposures — some with cassock, some in street clothes. Just request several glossy prints of each pose as you may require. These prints do not have to be "retouched" by the photographer. They will serve the newspaper's purpose without retouching. Do not request that the newspaper return your photo. You only make trouble for yourself and the newspaper. The cost to you of an unfinished glossy print is negligible.

A Reminder

Another source of publicity often neglected is your high school and college papers; your fraternity or honor society if you belonged to one; your fraternal publication, such as the K. of C. or other clubs in which you hold membership. These publications welcome news of their members, especially First Masses. They have no resources for gathering such information themselves. So give them the same copy and photographs you do the newspapers.

Souvenir Cards

It is customary for the newly ordained priest to distribute holy cards imprinted with his name and date of ordination or First Mass.

There are many samples readily available at the seminary and at religious-goods stores. The type selected and the inscription used are matters of individual taste. But use restraint in your printed message. The essential facts, without embellishments, make the most appropriate souvenirs. The quantity ordered and the distribution are optional. There are no rigid rules in these matters.

The only reason for mentioning the subject at all is a reminder to you that such cards should be selected and ordered well in advance, so as to assure delivery before your First Mass.

Gifts to You

Naturally your relatives and friends will wish to express their happiness at your First Mass by sending you presents. It is the accepted American way of sharing personally in your First Mass and in recognizing your honors.

Selecting an appropriate gift for you will not be an easy task for your friends. There are so few presents which are of practical use for you, the newly ordained priest.

It is no longer considered unconventional or improper to send the newly ordained a check. Today when parents or relatives, or even priests, are asked for information on the type of gift to be sent to the newly ordained they answer quite frankly: "There are so few things he needs, and these will be duplicated many times. Vestments, cassocks, or clothing are not practical gifts. Why not send him a check? Then he can combine his gifts and get something he really needs: his own chalice; a new typewriter; a tape recorder for his sermons; or something he may have looked forward to for several years."

Some of these gifts or checks will arrive before your First Mass, either at your home or to you personally. You *must* make a list of them immediately for acknowledgment, and instruct the folks at home to follow the same practice. (See below "Keep a List.")

Your Thanks for Gifts

It is an inflexible rule of society that gifts must be acknowledged promptly and personally. This rule applies with special force to you, the newly ordained priest. It is a sad fact and critical comment that this rule is flagrantly violated by thoughtless people and sometimes by priests, but you must not be classified with them.

If a friend thinks enough of you and your elevation to the priesthood to send you a congratulatory message or a Mass intention, or a present, you are honor bound by your office and by your social code to acknowledge it with a personal written message. You will never be excused by even your most intimate friends if you neglect this simple courtesy.

Keep a List

You must prepare yourself beforehand for this "thank you." Obtain a pocket-sized book in which you will jot down, as soon as they arrive, the gifts or checks and the names and addresses of the donors. You must instruct your relatives to do the same thing for gifts that are delivered to the house by mail or in person. Don't trust your memory! Keep a daily record.

Your Acknowledgments

Then, after your First Mass is over and the excitement subsides you must begin to acknowledge these congratulations and these gifts. You cannot delegate, or relegate, it to another. This duty is not transferable. You must perform it in person and by a personally written note. And it must be done promptly.

Convention makes only one concession to you. There are religious "thank you" cards and other appropriate religious note paper available in most Catholic goods stores which may be used for this purpose. The use of these cards is permissible today, but the message itself must be in your own handwriting.

The message must carry a personal intimate tone and the present (or check) must be mentioned by name. Here is where your little notebook serves its purpose. Do not mention the amount of the check, but you can write what you expect to do with it. Your "thank you" note need not be letter-length, but it must be personalized. You may end it with your priestly blessing or with a promise of a rememberance in your prayers and Masses.

Other Notes You Must Write

When the above obligations have been discharged, you still have two more duties to perform: You owe letters of thanks to all those who did so much to make your First Mass the wonderful event it was; and you owe little gifts to be given by *you* to others who assisted you in special ways. First your written messages.

The above procedure must also be followed for all congratulatory cards (without presents) which you receive. These notes may be brief but not curt, and they must be written in your own hand.

Letters of Thanks

You owe special thanks to many who helped you in various ways. Here is just a partial list to refresh your memory. These names, and others you will think of yourself, should be jotted down in your little book. You owe thanks to so many that you will forget someone if you do not mark these names down.

Suggestive List

The cathedral rector, where your ordination took place; the ordination retreat master; your pastor; the curates; the Sisters; the organist; the choir director and the choir; the head usher; the sacristan; the societies. Also, the priests who assisted you as ministers; your preacher; those who planned your dinner or reception; the Sisters and lay teachers of your school; others whose names will rise readily to your memory. All these names belong in your little notebook.

All these should receive your personally written letter or card of thanks, and others who helped in some special manner. Your own little memorandum book will contain the names of others to whom you are obligated. They must not be forgotten.

Your Gifts to Others

Your special *material* thanks should be given *by you* to others. For instance, the ministers who assisted you and your preacher should receive some tangible expression of your gratitude — a set of cuff links (they probably have a dozen sets already) or something personal for their desk, library, or hobby. To the altar boys should be given silver medals or rosaries, or something of a religious character.

To your own parents — your own love will dictate your gift to them; to your relatives to whom you are especially indebted for some feature of your celebration, and to others to whom you owe a debt of gratitude. Your own judgment will suggest gifts of an appropriate nature.

The major thought here is that you must not be entirely on the receiving end. Christ's admonition to His first Apostles was: "Freely you have received, freely give" (Mt 10:8).

Well Done!

It should be a labor of love to thank all these people. If you do so you will have the personal satisfaction that you have observed the conventionalities. You must, especially, be conscientious in acknowledging all gifts and congratulations that come from non-Catholics. To fail in this respect would be to neglect your new stewardship. To fulfill this social obligation will be a good start on your life of service to mankind. You will never know in this world how much your little thoughtful messages will have done for those who recieved them; you will never know what warmhearted thoughts they may have inspired in those people toward you and the priesthood you represent. You will be fulfilling your mission "Go into the whole world and preach — " and many a prayer may ascend heavenward for your stewardship.

"Put on therefore, as God's chosen ones, holy and beloved, a heart of mercy, kindness, humility, meakness, patience.

"Bear with one another and forgive one another, if anyone has a grievance against any other; even as the Lord has forgiven you, so also do you forgive.

"But above all these things have charity, which is the bond of perfection.

"And may the peace of Christ reign in your hearts; unto that peace, indeed, you were called in one body. Show yourselves thankful"

(Col 3:12–15).

Sources

Principal

New Esquire Etiquette for Men, Esquire Editors (Welch), Lippincott, 1959.

Additional

American Catholic Etiquette, Kay Toy Fenner, Newman Press, 1961.

Catholic Layman's Book of Etiquette, Robert C. Broderick, Catechetical Guild, 1957.

Christian Courtesy Series, Archdiocese of Chicago, School Board, 1958.

Clerical Etiquette, Joseph M. Connors, S.V.D. (mimeographed).

Complete Book of Etiquette, A. Vanderbilt, Doubleday & Co., 1957.

Courtesy for Clerics, Hermannus, Liverpool, London, 1950.

Courtesy in the Convent, The School Sisters of Notre Dame, Newman Press, 1952.

Emily Post's Etiquette, Funk & Wagnalls, 1957.

Praying in Public, Rev. Thomas Regis Murphy, The Bruce Publishing Co., 1959.

Priestly Practices, Arthur Barry O'Neill, C.S.C., Notre Dame Press, 1914.

Prophets of the Better Hope, Wm. J. Kerby, Bruce, 1946.

The Considerate Priest, Wm. J. Kerby, Catholic University Press, 1950.

The Gentlemanly Priest, Francis J. Connell, C.Ss.R., Grail, 1947.

The Voice With A Smile, Illinois Bell Telephone Company (pamphlet).

Today's Etiquette Questions Answered, A. Vanderbilt, Doubleday & Co., 1956.

INDEX